ARTS AND CRAFTS ACROSS THE
GRADE 1
CONTENTS

Language Arts Activities

Math Activities

Science Activities

Social Studies Activities

www.harcourtschoolsupply.com
© Harcourt Achieve Inc. All rights reserved.

Contents
Arts and Crafts Across the Curriculum 1, SV 1419023543

INTRODUCTION

Arts and Crafts Across the Curriculum is designed to provide arts and crafts activities that correlate with learning standards in the areas of language arts, math, science, and social studies. A wide variety of activities is presented throughout the book. Included are paintings, drawings, puppets, masks, mobiles, headbands, and much more. Regardless of the type of activity used, always allow for and encourage students' creativity.

Preparation for arts and crafts activities is made easier when the basic materials are easily accessible. Make materials such as glue, scissors, markers, crayons, and construction paper available for students to use. Allow plenty of time before doing an activity to collect materials such as paper plates, lunch sacks, or clothespins. Ask parents to help in the collection of recyclables such as paper towel tubes, tissue boxes, cereal boxes, lids, or empty water bottles.

Organization and Features

Each activity consists of two pages. The first page of each activity in the book includes the following:

- a specific standard in one of the core areas of learning which include language arts, math, science, or social studies
- several vocabulary words that students may become familiar with in relation to the topic of the activity
- background information that is related to the topic of the activity that can be discussed with students
- a drawing of the finished product to use as a reference

The second page of each activity includes the following:

- a list of materials needed to complete each activity
- step by step directions for teacher preparation
- step by step directions for the students to do in order to complete the activity
- several questions that the teacher can ask the students about the background information (may also be found on the first page)

In addition, the book contains

- reproducible patterns that are needed for specified activities
- a list of the learning standards referred to throughout the book
- an alphabetical index of the activities that are included in the book

2

www.harcourtschoolsupply.com
Introduction
Arts and Crafts Across the Curriculum 1, SV 1419023543

© Harcourt Achieve Inc. All rights reserved.

FIRST GRADE STANDARDS

Language Arts

- Knows alphabetical order of letters (pages 4–5)
- Identifies parts of a story (pages 6–7)
- Recognizes root words (pages 8–9)
- Makes illustrations to match sentences/stories (pages 10–11)
- Recognizes high-frequency sight words (pages 12–13)
- Recognizes nouns and verbs (pages 14–15)
- Identifies the parts of a book (pages 16–17)
- Recognizes beginning consonants (pages 18–19)

Math

- Recognizes money and counts amounts using penny, nickel, dime, and quarter (pages 20–21)
- Counts by 5's (pages 22–23)
- Measures length using nonstandard units (pages 24–25)
- Identifies fractions $\frac{1}{4}$, $\frac{1}{3}$, and $\frac{1}{2}$ (pages 26–27)
- Tells time by the hour and half-hour (pages 28–29)
- Creates and extends a pattern (pages 30–31)
- Counts and recognizes numbers to 100 (pages 32–33)
- Knows basic addition facts (pages 34–35)

Science

- Observes the life cycle of organisms (pages 36–37)
- Observes and describes differences in rocks (pages 38–39)
- Identifies characteristics of living organisms (pages 40–41, 48–49)
- Observes and records changes in the weather (pages 42–43)
- Observes, describes, and records changes in position (pages 44–55)
- Identifies basic needs of living organisms (pages 46–47)
- Observes and describes the parts of plants (pages 50–51)
- Identifies basic food groups (pages 52–53)
- Studies habitat, structure, and behavior of animals (pages 54–55)
- Understands the properties of earth materials (pages 56–57)
- Observes the life cycle of organisms (pages 58–59)

Social Studies

- Identifies the contributions of historical figures that helped to shape our nation (pages 60–61)
- Identifies leaders in the community, state, and nation (pages 62–63)
- Identifies places to acquire basic goods and services (pages 64–65)
- Identifies customs associated with national patriotic holidays (pages 66–67)
- Identifies Earth's features on maps, such as rivers, oceans, and mountains (pages 68–69)
- Compares and contrasts a farm and a city (pages 70–71)
- Discusses ways people can take care of the environment (pages 72–73)
- Describes past forms of communication (pages 74–75)
- Compares family customs and traditions (pages 76–77)
- Identifies ordinary people who helped shape the community (pages 78–79)
- Discusses how various groups have gained or lost political freedom (pages 80–81)
- Describes national patriotic symbols (pages 82–83)

www.harcourtschoolsupply.com
© Harcourt Achieve Inc. All rights reserved.

ABC GARDEN CART

Language Arts Standard
Knows alphabetical
order of letters

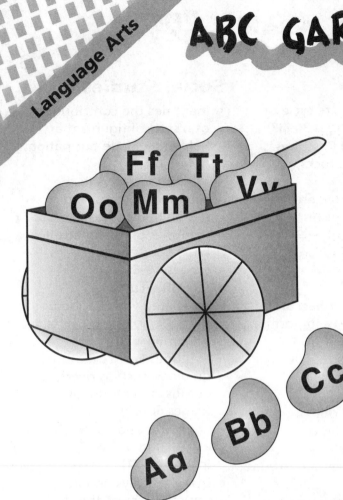

Vocabulary

cart
wheels
seeds
alphabet
sequence

Discussion

- A cart is a vehicle that is used to transport items and usually has two wheels.
- Seeds are the part of a plant that can grow a new plant if the environmental conditions are right.
- There are twenty-six letters in the alphabet.
- Each letter can be written with a capital letter and a lowercase letter.
- The letters of the alphabet are arranged in a certain sequence or order.

www.harcourtschoolsupply.com
© Harcourt Achieve Inc. All rights reserved.

Materials

- patterns on page 84
- one plastic laundry scoop per student
- baby food jar lid for a template
- old file folders
- yellow construction paper
- markers
- scissors
- glue

Directions

Teacher Preparation

1. Duplicate the seed pattern and use it to make a template on a file folder.
2. Trace the seed template on folded yellow construction paper.
3. Cut out several seeds at a time. Repeat until each student has 26 seeds.

Student Directions

1. Use the baby food jar lid as a template and trace two circles on a file folder.
2. Cut the two circles out for the wheels on the cart.
3. Draw spokes on the wheels.
4. Glue the wheels on the sides of the laundry scoop so that it resembles a cart.
5. Write the letters of the alphabet on 26 seeds.
6. Place the seeds in the cart and mix them up.
7. Remove the seeds from the cart and line them up on the table in alphabetical order.
8. Store the seeds in the cart.

Questions

1. What is the difference between a wagon and a cart? (A wagon has four wheels, and a cart can have two wheels.)
2. What is a cart used for? (to carry and move things)
3. How many letters are in the alphabet? (twenty-six)
4. Which letter is tenth in alphabetical sequence? (Jj)
5. Which letter is nineteenth in alphabetical sequence? (Ss)

www.harcourtschoolsupply.com
© Harcourt Achieve Inc. All rights reserved.

Language Arts Activities
Arts and Crafts Across the Curriculum 1, SV 1419023543

PARTS OF A STORY BOX

The animals chased the Gingerbread Man.

Vocabulary

characters
setting
plot
problem
conclusion

Discussion

- Every story has the same basic parts including character(s), a plot, and a setting.
- Stories have a main character or characters and sometimes other supporting characters.
- The characters can be adults, children, animals, or objects. Animals or objects can be given human traits such as in *The Gingerbread Man* story.
- The plot of the story tells what happened to the character or characters and includes some kind of problem, conflict, or adventure.
- Stories have a beginning, middle, and ending. The ending is the conclusion of the story.
- The setting is where the story takes place and includes a time period which tells when the story took place.

www.harcourtschoolsupply.com
© Harcourt Achieve Inc. All rights reserved.

Language Arts Activities
Arts and Crafts Across the Curriculum 1, SV 1419023543

Materials

- one empty cube-shaped tissue box per student
- jumbo craft sticks
- white construction paper
- retractable utility knife
- ruler
- markers
- scissors
- glue

Directions

Teacher Preparation
1. Cut the bottom off of the tissue boxes using the knife.
2. Measure the side of the tissue box and cut the white construction paper to fit. Provide four pieces for each student.

Student Directions
1. Select and read a favorite story.
2. Write or dictate the title of the story on a square piece of paper.
3. Glue the paper on one side of the tissue box.
4. Write or dictate a sentence telling about the plot of the story.
5. Glue it on a second side of the tissue box.
6. Repeat the procedure and tell about the setting of the story.
7. On the last side of the box, tell about the conclusion of the story.
8. Use construction paper, markers, and craft sticks to create a stick puppet of the main character in the story.
9. If time allows, make stick puppets for the other characters in the story.
10. Insert the puppets up through the bottom of the tissue box so that they appear out of the top opening and retell the story.

Questions

1. Name the three basic parts of a story. (character, plot, and setting)
2. Who or what is a character? (who or what the story is about)
3. What is the plot of a story? (It tells what happened to the character or characters.)
4. When in a story does the conclusion occur? (at the end)
5. Where a story takes place is called the what? (the setting)

7

© Harcourt Achieve Inc. All rights reserved.

TUBE TREE WITH ROOT WORDS

Language Arts Standard
Recognizes root words

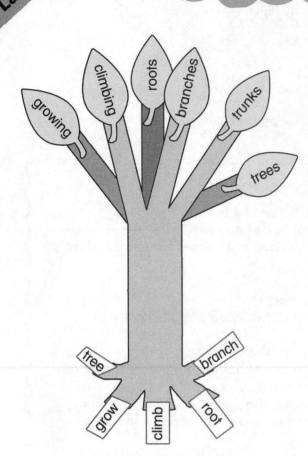

Vocabulary
tree
leaves
branches
trunk
roots

Discussion

- The leaves are attached to the branches of the tree and capture sunlight.
- Leaves use the energy from the sun to feed the tree.
- Branches connect the trunk to the leaves and provide the leaves with water.
- The roots on a tree anchor the tree in the ground and absorb water, nutrients, and minerals from the soil.
- The root is the main part of a word to which small word parts are added.

© Harcourt Achieve Inc. All rights reserved.
Arts and Crafts Across the Curriculum 1, SV 1419023543

Materials

- patterns on page 84
- one paper towel tube per child
- white paper
- green construction paper
- chart
- pencils
- scissors
- glue

Directions

Teacher Preparation

1. Duplicate six leaves per student on green construction paper.
2. Make six one-inch cuts that are evenly spaced around the bottom end of the tube and bend the pieces out to resemble the roots of a tree.
3. Make six three-inch cuts that are evenly spaced around the top end of the tube and bend the pieces out to resemble the branches of a tree.
4. Cut six one-by-two-inch strips of white paper for each student.
5. Make a chart with words such as *trees, branches, roots, trunks, growing,* and *planted.*

Student Directions

1. Cut out six leaves.
2. Write a word from the chart on each leaf.
3. Glue a leaf on each branch of the tube tree.
4. Write each root word on a strip of white paper.
5. Glue one strip of paper on each root of the tube tree.

Questions

1. What is the root of a word? (the main part)
2. Name two functions of tree roots. (They hold the tree in the ground and absorb water and nutrients.)
3. What part of the tree are the leaves attached to? (the branches)
4. Which part makes food for the tree? (the leaves)
5. What do leaves need in order to start the process of making food for the tree? (sunlight)

www.harcourtschoolsupply.com
© Harcourt Achieve Inc. All rights reserved.

FILE FOLDER FRAMES

Language Arts Standard
Makes illustrations to
match sentences/stories

The pig sat under the tree.

Vocabulary

pig
boar
sow
piglet
mammal

Discussion

- A father pig is called a boar, a mother is a sow, and a baby is a piglet.
- A sow can give birth to 8 to 12 piglets in one litter.
- Pigs have four toes on each foot but walk on only two on each foot, which makes it look like they are walking on tiptoe.
- Pigs are the only mammal without sweat glands. They roll in the mud to cool off during hot weather.
- Pigs have a keen sense of smell and spend much of their time rooting for tidbits of food.

www.harcourtschoolsupply.com
© Harcourt Achieve Inc. All rights reserved.

Materials

- one old file folder per student
- several stories about pigs
- white copy paper
- ruler
- stapler
- markers
- scissors
- glue
- pencils

Directions

Teacher Preparation

1. Cut off the tabs of the folders so that the top has a straight edge.
2. Measure a 6" x 9" section on the front side of the folder leaving a wider edge at the bottom than at the top.
3. Cut out the measured section to form a frame.
4. When students have completed their illustration, staple the sides and top of the folder together.

Student Directions

1. Read a pig story.
2. Write a sentence across the bottom edge of the folder frame that tells about one part of the story.
3. Draw and color an illustration of the sentence on a sheet of white paper.
4. Glue the illustration on the inside of the folder so that it shows through the frame opening.
5. Have an adult help staple the sides and the top of the folder together.
6. Use markers to decorate the edge of the frame.

Questions

1. What is a mother pig called? (sow)
2. What is a baby pig called? (piglet)
3. How do pigs cool off? (roll in the mud)
4. What are pigs looking for when they are rooting? (food)
5. How many toes does a pig have? (four)

www.harcourtschoolsupply.com
© Harcourt Achieve Inc. All rights reserved.

STAND-UP SQUIRREL

Language Arts Standard
Recognizes high-frequency sight words

Vocabulary
sight words
high-frequency
squirrel
acorns
leaps

THE LITTLE SQUIRREL

We saw a little squirrel
Climbing up a tree.
He held up his acorn
For all of us to see.

Discussion

- High-frequency words are the 100 to 300 most common sight words. Sight words are those that must be recognized at a glance.
- The squirrel's diet consists of nuts, seeds, and fruit.
- Squirrels chew on branches of the tree to sharpen and clean their teeth.
- Squirrels do not hibernate but store great quantities of food for the winter.
- A squirrel uses its tail for balancing as it leaps from tree to tree and also uses it as a blanket to wrap around itself in cold weather.
- The eyes of squirrels are located high on their head so that they can see in front of and behind them.

www.harcourtschoolsupply.com
© Harcourt Achieve Inc. All rights reserved.

Language Arts Activities
Arts and Crafts Across the Curriculum 1, SV 1419023543

Materials

- patterns on page 85
- one brown bathroom tissue roll per student
- brown construction paper
- small paper cups
- brown tissue paper
- pencils
- markers
- scissors
- glue

Directions

Teacher Preparation

1. Duplicate a squirrel head, tail, and body on brown construction paper for each student.
2. Duplicate a generous supply of acorns on brown construction paper.
3. Cut brown tissue paper into eight-inch squares.

Student Directions

1. Cut out the head, tail, and body of the squirrel.
2. Wrap the body around the tube and glue it in place.
3. Curl the tail by rolling it around a pencil.
4. Glue it to the back of the squirrel.
5. Glue the head to the top of the tube.
6. Place a small paper cup in the center of a tissue paper square. Lift up the edges and tuck them inside the cup so that it resembles a basket.
7. Cut out several acorns and write a high-frequency word on each one.
8. Place them in the "basket" in front of the squirrel.
9. Take out each acorn and practice reading the words.

Questions

1. Describe two ways a squirrel uses its tail. (for balance and warmth)
2. What kind of food does a squirrel eat? (nuts, seeds, fruit)
3. Why are the eyes of squirrels located high on their head? (so they can see in front of and behind them)
4. Write all of the high-frequency sight words in the poem on page 12. (Answers will vary.)
5. Which high-frequency sight words are used twice in the poem? (up, a)

www.harcourtschoolsupply.com
© Harcourt Achieve Inc. All rights reserved.

TUBE BUTTERFLY

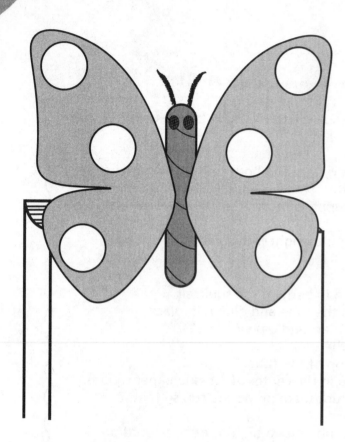

Vocabulary
butterfly
insect
scales
noun
verb

Discussion

- Butterflies are flying insects with large, scaly wings.
- They have two pairs of wings that are covered with colorful, iridescent scales that are in overlapping rows.
- The design or pattern on both of the butterfly's wings is symmetrical.
- A butterfly has a strawlike mouth called a proboscis.
- A noun is a part of speech that includes the name of a person, place, or thing.
- A verb is a part of speech that usually indicates an action.

www.harcourtschoolsupply.com
© Harcourt Achieve Inc. All rights reserved.

Language Arts Activities
Arts and Crafts Across the Curriculum 1, SV 1419023543

Materials

- patterns on page 86
- one paper towel tube per student
- black tempera paint
- paintbrushes
- white construction paper
- black pipe cleaners
- paint shirts or aprons
- markers
- stapler
- scissors
- glue

Directions

Teacher Preparation

1. Duplicate on white construction paper two wings and the noun and verb pictures for each student.
2. Press the ends of the paper towel tube flat and cut a rounded curve on both ends.
3. Staple one end flat.
4. On the other end cut a two- to three-inch slit on each side.
5. Prepare a paint station with black paint.
6. Cut the pipe cleaners into quarters so that each student has two pieces.
7. When the butterfly is completed, help students staple two pipe cleaners on the head for antennae.

Student Directions

1. Paint the tube black to resemble the head, thorax, and abdomen of a butterfly. Set aside to dry.
2. Decorate the two butterfly wings with markers, making them symmetrical.
3. Cut out the six pictures of nouns and verbs.
4. Glue all of the nouns on the left wing.
5. Glue all of the verbs on the right wing.
6. Glue the wings on the middle of the tube with the stapled end at the top.
7. Draw eyes on the butterfly.
8. Have an adult staple two pipe cleaners on the head to resemble antennae.
9. Put the butterfly over the cover of a book using the slits on the sides.

Questions

1. What are butterfly wings covered with? (scales)
2. How many pairs of wings does a butterfly have? (two pair)
3. What is the strawlike mouth of a butterfly called? (proboscis)
4. Name the noun in the sentence *The butterfly flew.* (butterfly)

www.harcourtschoolsupply.com
© Harcourt Achieve Inc. All rights reserved.

Language Arts Activities
Arts and Crafts Across the Curriculum 1, SV 1419023543

PARTS OF A BOOK BUBBLE PRINTS

Language Arts Standard
Identifies the parts of a book

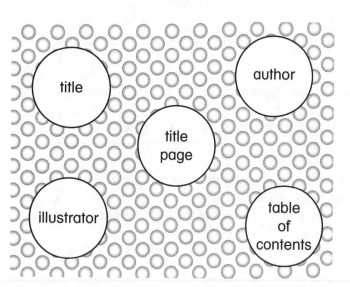

Vocabulary
title
author
illustrator
title page
table of contents

Discussion

- The name of a book is called the title. The title is shown on the spine, the front cover of the book, and on the title page.
- The author is the name of the person or persons who wrote the book.
- The illustrator is the name of the person who drew the illustrations or pictures in the book.
- The title page is the first page in the book and tells the name of the book, the author, the illustrator, and the company that published the book.
- The table of contents in a book lists the title, the number of chapters, and the page numbers of all the chapters in a book. It is used to find information quickly.

www.harcourtschoolsupply.com
© Harcourt Achieve Inc. All rights reserved.

Language Arts Activities
Arts and Crafts Across the Curriculum 1, SV 1419023543

Materials

- white construction paper
- plastic wrap with bubbles
- 2½" lid for use as a template
- old file folders
- tempera paint
- paintbrush
- scissors
- old cookie sheet
- masking tape
- paint shirts or aprons
- pencils

Directions

Teacher Preparation

1. Cut a piece of plastic wrap that is slightly larger than the construction paper.
2. Tape the plastic wrap to the cookie sheet with masking tape.
3. Prepare a station for the paint.
4. Trace the shape of the lid on a file folder five times for each student.
5. Cut out the five circles.
6. Stick a loop of masking tape on each circle.

Student Directions

1. Wear a paint shirt or apron.
2. Tape the five circles on the white paper where desired. Lay the paper to the side.
3. Cover the plastic wrap with paint.
4. Turn the white paper facedown on the plastic wrap.
5. Rub across the paper a few times.
6. Gently remove the paper from the plastic wrap.
7. Remove the taped circles and allow the paint to dry.
8. In the white areas, write the parts of a book which include the title, author, illustrator, title page, and table of contents.

Questions

1. What is the name of a book? (the title)
2. What is the name of the person who wrote the book? (the author)
3. Who draws the pictures in a book? (the illustrator)
4. Where in the book is the title page found? (the first page)
5. What information is found in the table of contents? (the title, the number of chapters, and the pages of the chapters)

www.harcourtschoolsupply.com
© Harcourt Achieve Inc. All rights reserved.

CONSONANT EGG CARTON GAME

Language Arts Standard
Recognizes beginning consonants

Vocabulary

consonant
vowel
digraph
phonics
phoneme

Discussion

- Phonics is the study of the way in which spellings represent the sounds that make up words.
- An individual sound unit of speech is called a phoneme.
- A consonant is a sound formed by stopping the air flowing through the mouth.
- There are twenty-one consonants in the English language.
- *Y* is a consonant when used at the beginning of a word.
- Two consonants that are paired together to represent a single speech sound are called a digraph.

www.harcourtschoolsupply.com
© Harcourt Achieve Inc. All rights reserved.

Language Arts Activities
Arts and Crafts Across the Curriculum 1, SV 1419023543

Materials

- one foam egg carton per student
- construction paper
- large lima beans
- writing paper
- pencils
- markers
- scissors
- glue

Directions

Teacher Preparation

1. Cut off the front flap of the egg cartons.
2. Cut two three-by-five-inch pieces of construction paper for each student.

Student Directions

1. Glue two pieces of construction paper on the inside of the lid.
2. Decorate the inside of the egg carton lid using construction paper.
3. Write one consonant in the bottom of each cup of the carton.
4. Set the open carton on the floor with the lid propped against a solid surface such as a wall.
5. Stand a few feet from the carton.
6. Toss a lima bean into the egg carton.
7. Name the consonant on which it lands.
8. Write a word that begins with that sound on the writing paper.
9. Continue playing for a predetermined amount of time.

Questions

1. How many consonants are in the alphabet? (twenty-one)
2. Which consonant is sometimes used as a vowel? (*y*)
3. Name two words that begin with the consonant sound of /b/. (Answers will vary.)
4. Which two consonant sounds does the letter *g* make? (/g/ as in *goat* and /g/ as in *giraffe*)
5. Does the consonant sound /d/ come at the beginning or ending of the word *bed*? (ending)

19

© Harcourt Achieve Inc. All rights reserved.

MONEY CANS

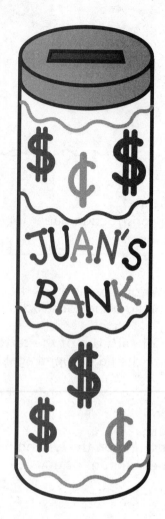

Vocabulary

coins
penny
nickel
dime
quarter

Discussion

- Money is used to buy goods and services.
- A penny is worth one cent.
- A nickel is worth five cents.
- A dime is worth ten cents.
- A quarter is worth twenty-five cents.

20

Materials

- one empty potato chip can with a lid per student
- white construction paper
- stickers
- collection of coins
- retractable utility knife
- markers
- scissors
- glue

Directions

Teacher Preparation

1. Use the knife to cut a coin slot in the plastic lids.
2. Cut the construction paper to fit the height and circumference of the cans.

Student Directions

1. Write your name and the word *bank* with markers. For example, write *Juan's Bank*. Make it fancy and colorful.
2. Draw a decorative border on the top and bottom edge of the construction paper.
3. Cover the paper with dollar and cents signs and stickers.
4. Glue the construction paper to fit around the can.
5. Save a collection of coins in the can.
6. Remove the lid and take out a small handful of coins.
7. Count how much money you take out of the can.
8. Replace coins, shake the can, and repeat the procedure.

Questions

1. How many cents is a penny worth? A nickel? A dime? A quarter? (one cent, five cents, ten cents, twenty-five cents)
2. How many cents does one dime and three pennies make? (thirteen cents)
3. How much are two dimes worth? (twenty cents)
4. Name two ways to make twenty five cents. (Answers will vary.)
5. How many nickels does it take to make a quarter? (five)

21

CEREAL BOX ANTHILL

Math Standard
Counts by 5's

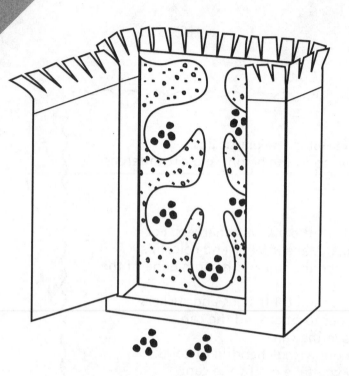

Vocabulary
ant
queen
chamber
tunnels
colony

Discussion

- Ants are social insects, which means they live in organized colonies.
- The main function of the colony is to provide protection and food for the queen.
- Many ants build their nests underground in soil, but some build nests in trees or under leaves.
- Underground nests usually consist of horizontal chambers that are connected by tunnels.
- Each chamber has a specific function such as caring for the queen, caring for the young, food storage, or discarding garbage.

www.harcourtschoolsupply.com
© Harcourt Achieve Inc. All rights reserved.

Math Activities
Arts and Crafts Across the Curriculum 1, SV 1419023543

Materials

- pattern on page 87
- one cereal box per student
- green construction paper
- brown tempera paint
- paintbrushes
- paint shirts or aprons
- one package black beans
- glue
- markers or crayons
- scissors

Directions

Teacher Preparation

1. Duplicate the anthill for each student.
2. Cut the flaps off of the open end of the cereal box.
3. On the front of the box, cut down and then across to form a "door." Fold the piece back.
4. Prepare a station with brown paint.
5. Cut green construction paper into three-inch strips.

Student Directions

1. Put on a paint shirt or apron.
2. Paint the front and two sides of the cereal box brown and set it aside to dry.
3. Fringe the green paper to look like grass.
4. Glue paper grass completely around the top edge of the box.
5. Color the chambers of the anthill black and the background brown.
6. Cut out the anthill.
7. Glue five black beans in each chamber to resemble ants.
8. Glue the anthill on the inside back of the box so that the "door" can be opened to see underground.
9. Count the ants by 5's.
10. Continue making sets of 5 "ants" to reach a total of 100 ants. Place the sets on a table.

Questions

1. Which ant do all of the other ants take care of? (the queen)
2. Where do many ants build their nest? (underground)
3. What is the part of the anthill called that is like a little room? (a chamber)
4. What connects the chambers in the anthill? (tunnels)
5. Name two ways the chambers are used. (Answers will vary.)

www.harcourtschoolsupply.com
© Harcourt Achieve Inc. All rights reserved.

PAPER PLATE TURTLES

Math Standard
Measures length using
nonstandard units

Vocabulary
reptiles
scales
loggerhead turtles
nest

Discussion

- Reptiles, including turtles and tortoises, are coldblooded vertebrates that breathe air with lungs and are covered with scales. Their backbone is attached to the shell.
- Loggerheads, whose name refers to their large head, are one of the most common types of sea turtles.
- Sea turtles spend their life in the ocean except when the females leave the water to lay their eggs on the beach.
- The female digs a nest cavity 18–22 inches deep.
- She then lays approximately 100 eggs the size of table tennis balls, covers the nest with sand, and returns to the water.

www.harcourtschoolsupply.com
© Harcourt Achieve Inc. All rights reserved.

Math Activities
Arts and Crafts Across the Curriculum 1, SV 1419023543

Materials

- patterns on page 88
- paper plates
- green construction paper
- one-inch brads
- hole punch
- crayons
- scissors
- glue

Directions

Teacher Preparation

1. Duplicate the head, legs, and tail on green construction paper. Provide each student with two front and two hind legs.
2. Ask the question, *"How many turtles wide is the classroom?"*
3. When the turtles are completed, help students lay them end to end to measure the width of the classroom.

Student Directions

1. Color the bottom side of the paper plate green.
2. Draw large scales with a black crayon for the shell of the turtle.
3. Cut out the head, four legs, and the tail.
4. Punch one hole for the head and four holes for the legs around the edge of the plate.
5. Attach the head and four legs with the brads so that they can move from side to side.
6. Glue the tail between the two back legs.

Questions

1. What are reptiles covered with? (scales)
2. Where do loggerhead turtles spend their lives? (in the ocean)
3. Where do female loggerhead turtles lay their eggs? (on the beach)
4. About how many eggs does a mother turtle lay? (about 100)
5. What size are the eggs? (the size of a table tennis ball)

www.harcourtschoolsupply.com
© Harcourt Achieve Inc. All rights reserved.

Math Activities
Arts and Crafts Across the Curriculum 1, SV 1419023543

FRACTION ART

Math Standard
Identifies fractions $\frac{1}{4}$, $\frac{1}{3}$, and $\frac{1}{2}$

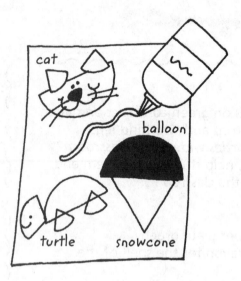

Vocabulary

fraction

whole

half

equal

part

Discussion

- A fraction is any part of a whole unit or one number divided by another number.
- Fractions are used by people because they are often the easiest way to represent some quantity.
- *Equal* means the same amount in all parts.
- The top number of a fraction is called the numerator and is the number of equal parts out of the whole.
- The bottom number is called the denominator and indicates the number of parts in which the whole is divided.

www.harcourtschoolsupply.com
© Harcourt Achieve Inc. All rights reserved.

Math Activities
Arts and Crafts Across the Curriculum 1, SV 1419023543

Materials

- one envelope per student
- one small butter tub lid for use as a template
- manila paper
- various colors of construction paper
- paper cutter
- crayons
- pencils
- scissors
- glue

Directions

Teacher Preparation

1. Trace and cut out two circles from any color of construction paper per student.
2. Use the paper cutter to cut two of each of the following shapes for each student:
   - four-inch rectangles
   - three-inch squares
   - three-inch equilateral triangles
3. Write on each square or rectangle a fraction such as $\frac{1}{4}$, $\frac{1}{3}$, or $\frac{1}{2}$ to indicate how many pieces in which to cut it.
4. Write on each circle the fraction $\frac{1}{4}$ or $\frac{1}{2}$ to indicate how many pieces in which to cut it.
5. Write on each triangle the fraction $\frac{1}{2}$ to indicate how many pieces in which to cut it.
6. Put a set of shapes in an envelope for each student.

Student Directions

1. Read the fractions on each shape.
2. Cut each shape into the equal parts as indicated.
3. Use the fraction pieces to construct pictures.
4. Glue the pieces on a sheet of manila paper.
5. Write a label for each picture.

Questions

1. What does it mean to divide an object into equal parts? (All parts are the same.)
2. What does the bottom number of a fraction tell? (how many parts in which the whole is divided)
3. What does the top number of a fraction tell? (the number of equal parts out of the whole)
4. How would one-half be written? (one on top and two on the bottom)
5. There are four cookies. How many cookies would Billy get if he got half of them? (two)

27

www.harcourtschoolsupply.com
© Harcourt Achieve Inc. All rights reserved.

LADYBUG CLOCK

Math Standard
Tells time by the
hour and half-hour

Vocabulary

time
clock
ladybug
aphids
beetle

Discussion

- A clock measures time in hours, minutes, and seconds.
- On an analog clock, the hour hand is shorter than the minute hand.
- The ladybug is a type of beetle. Beetles are insects.
- The most common ladybug is red with black spots.
- The number of spots identifies the type of ladybug. There are over 5,000 species of ladybugs in the world.
- Ladybugs are welcome in gardens since they eat pests such as aphids. They can eat 25–50 aphids a day.
- A ladybug beats its wings 85 times a minute when it flies.

www.harcourtschoolsupply.com
© Harcourt Achieve Inc. All rights reserved.

Math Activities
Arts and Crafts Across the Curriculum 1, SV 1419023543

Materials

- patterns on page 89
- a copy of the book *The Grouchy Ladybug* by Eric Carle
- two paper plates per student
- black construction paper
- black pipe cleaners
- large wiggly eyes
- brads

- red and black tempera paint
- paintbrushes
- paint shirts or aprons
- hole punch

- crayons or markers
- scissors
- glue
- ruler

Directions

Teacher Preparation

1. Duplicate the clock face and hands for each student.
2. Cut pipe cleaners into two-inch sections.
3. Prepare a paint station for the red and black paint.

Student Directions

1. Read *The Grouchy Ladybug* and look at the clocks on each page.
2. Paint about one-fourth of the paper plate black.
3. Paint the remaining part of the plate red. Set it aside to dry.
4. Color and cut out the clock hands and the clock face.
5. Glue the clock face on the unpainted side of the paper plate.
6. Attach the clock hands with a brad.
7. Punch two holes and attach pipe cleaners to the head for antennae.
8. Glue two wiggly eyes on the head.
9. Draw a black line down the middle of the ladybug's back for the wings.
10. Paint black dots on the ladybug. Paint a black dot over the brad prongs to camouflage the brad.
11. Use the clock to practice telling time.

Questions

1. On what number does the minute hand point for every hour? (the twelve) For the half hour? (the six)
2. What is the most common color of ladybug? (red with black spots)
3. What type of animal is a ladybug? (an insect)
4. Why do people like ladybugs in their garden? (They eat pests like aphids.)
5. How many times a minute do a ladybug's wings beat when it flies? (85 times)

www.harcourtschoolsupply.com
© Harcourt Achieve Inc. All rights reserved.

Math Activities
Arts and Crafts Across the Curriculum 1, SV 1419023543

PATTERNED AQUARIUM ART

Math Standard
Creates and extends a pattern

Vocabulary
goldfish
aquarium
pet
oxygen
gills

Discussion

- Goldfish are the most common household pets.
- Goldfish live in tanks with fresh water. The more surface area the tank has the better it is for the fish.
- Goldfish are quite intelligent and can recognize the person who feeds them. They swim back and forth when they are about to be fed.
- Goldfish like to play and need exercise, so two fish are better than one in a tank.
- Fish are vertebrates whose bodies are covered with scales.
- Fish need oxygen to stay alive and use their gills to remove the oxygen from the water.

www.harcourtschoolsupply.com
© Harcourt Achieve Inc. All rights reserved.

Math Activities
Arts and Crafts Across the Curriculum 1, SV 1419023543

Materials

- one cereal box per student
- laminating film scraps or plastic wrap
- white construction paper
- blue watercolor paint
- paintbrushes
- glue
- crayons
- various colors of construction paper
- paint shirts or aprons
- masking tape
- scissors

Directions

Teacher Preparation

1. Cut out the front of the cereal box, leaving about a one-inch border.
2. Cut the white construction paper to match the size of the box.
3. Cut a generous supply of all colors of construction paper into one-inch squares.
4. When students have completed their pictures, help them tape laminating film or plastic wrap on the box to cover the opening in order to resemble the glass of an aquarium.

Student Directions

1. Draw a picture of a goldfish with crayons on white construction paper. Add some rocks or sand at the bottom and some seaweed. Press hard with the crayons.
2. Paint all of the construction paper with blue watercolors, including the fish.
3. Glue the picture on the inside of the cereal box so that it can be seen through the opening.
4. Have an adult help tape laminating film or plastic wrap on the box to cover the opening in order to resemble the glass of an aquarium.
5. Glue one-inch squares of construction paper around the edge of the box in a pattern.

Questions

1. What animal is the most common household pet? (the goldfish)
2. Do goldfish live in fresh or salt water? (fresh)
3. How do goldfish show their intelligence? (They recognize who feeds them.)
4. What are the bodies of fish covered with? (scales)
5. How do goldfish breathe in the water? (Their gills remove the oxygen from the water.)

31

© Harcourt Achieve Inc. All rights reserved.

HAPPY 100 HAT

Math Standard
Counts and recognizes
numbers to 100

Vocabulary

hundred
century
dollar
Celsius
senators
Congress

Discussion

- *Centi* is the prefix meaning *hundred*.
- One hundred years make a century.
- One hundred cents equal one dollar.
- Ten sets of ten objects is a way of making a hundred.
- The boiling point for water in the metric system is 100° Celsius.
- There are 100 senators in Congress. Two senators represent each state.

32

Materials

- one sentence strip per student
- various colors of construction paper
- glitter
- small objects such as beans, stickers, or beads
- paper cutter
- stapler
- lid from a small butter tub
- scissors
- glue
- tape measure
- pencils

Directions

Teacher Preparation

1. Use the paper cutter to cut one-by-twelve-inch strips of construction paper. Provide each student with ten strips.
2. Provide each student with a sheet of construction paper that has been cut in half lengthwise.
3. Help measure each student's head and staple the sentence strip hat to fit.
4. Help staple the ten strips around the hat.

Student Directions

1. Fold the sentence strip in half to find the center and mark it with a pencil.
2. Cut out the number 100 from construction paper. Trace the lid to make two zeroes.
3. Glue the 100 on the sentence strip where the center is marked.
4. Spread a thin layer of glue on the numbers and sprinkle with glitter.
5. Have an adult help measure your head and staple the sentence strip hat to fit.
6. Glue ten items on each of ten paper strips.
7. Have an adult help staple the ten strips around the hat to make 100.

Questions

1. What is a period of a hundred years called? (a century)
2. How many cents are in a dollar? (one hundred)
3. How many sets of ten make a hundred? (ten)
4. Why is the number 100 important on the Celsius thermometer? (It is the boiling point of water.)
5. How is the number 100 used in Congress? (It is the number of senators.)

33

www.harcourtschoolsupply.com
Math Activities
Arts and Crafts Across the Curriculum 1, SV 1419023543
© Harcourt Achieve Inc. All rights reserved.

ELEPHANT ADDITION CAN

Math Standard
Knows basic addition facts

Vocabulary

elephant
mammal
herd
memory
addition

Discussion

- Elephants are the largest mammals in the world that live on land.
- Several families of elephants live together in a "herd."
- The leader of the herd is usually the oldest female elephant.
- Elephants are plant-eaters that spend as much as twenty hours a day eating.
- Elephants have good memories. Remembering where to find food and water in times of drought helps them survive in the wild.
- Elephants cool themselves when it is hot by using their trunks to spray themselves with water or dust.
- One way in which humans use their memory is to remember addition facts.
- Addition is the total amount of two or more numbers.

www.harcourtschoolsupply.com
© Harcourt Achieve Inc. All rights reserved.

Math Activities
Arts and Crafts Across the Curriculum 1, SV 1419023543

Materials

- one 15-ounce juice can per student
- gray construction paper
- craft sticks
- a four-inch plastic lid
- a three-inch plastic lid
- wiggly eyes
- writing paper
- pencils
- black markers
- scissors
- glue

Directions

Teacher Preparation

1. Cut gray construction paper for each student to fit the height and circumference of the juice can.
2. Cut a one-by-six-inch strip of gray paper for each student.

Student Directions

1. Glue gray construction paper around the juice can.
2. Trace and cut out one four-inch circle and two three-inch circles on gray construction paper.
3. Glue the smaller circles slightly behind the large circle to resemble the ears of an elephant.
4. Glue two wiggly eyes and draw a mouth on the large circle.
5. Fold a one-by-six-inch strip of gray paper in accordion pleats for the trunk of the elephant.
6. Glue the trunk above the mouth.
7. Glue the head of the elephant to the side of the juice can.
8. Write the numbers 0–9 on ten craft sticks. Repeat to make a second set.
9. Put all twenty sticks in the can and mix them up.
10. Remove two sticks from the can and find the sum of the two numbers.
11. Write the equation on writing paper.

Questions

1. What is the largest mammal that lives on land? (the elephant)
2. What is a group of elephants that live together called? (a herd)
3. Which elephant is the leader of the herd? (the oldest female elephant)
4. How do elephants cool themselves when it is hot? (They use their trunks to spray themselves with water or dust.)
5. What is addition the total amount of? (two or more numbers)

35

www.harcourtschoolsupply.com
© Harcourt Achieve Inc. All rights reserved.

BALLOON SPIDERLINGS

Science Standard
Observes the life cycle
of organisms

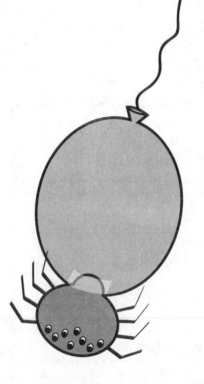

Vocabulary

egg sac
spiderlings
ballooning
spinnerets
silk

Discussion

- A female spider lays up to 500 sticky eggs. She then wraps them with silk to form an egg sac.
- The baby spiders, called spiderlings, remain in or around the egg sac until they have molted once.
- Many spiderlings leave their place of birth by ballooning.
- Ballooning is when they climb to a high place, tip their abdomen upward, and release a strand of silk from their spinnerets.
- The breeze picks the strand of silk up and carries the spiderling along like a balloon.

www.harcourtschoolsupply.com
© Harcourt Achieve Inc. All rights reserved.

Science Activities
Arts and Crafts Across the Curriculum 1, SV 1419023543

Materials

- white string
- one small black balloon per student
- black construction paper
- black pipe cleaners
- chalk
- three-inch plastic lid
- tape
- scissors
- glue
- stapler

Directions

Teacher Preparation

1. Cut enough pipe cleaners in half so that each student has four halves.
2. Help students blow up a balloon and tie it.
3. Tie a one- to two-foot piece of string to each balloon.
4. Help students staple the circles together leaving the folded sections open.

Student Directions

1. Use the plastic lid to trace and cut out two three-inch circles from black construction paper.
2. Lay four pipe cleaners across the middle of one circle and tape them in place.
3. Fold a small section of the circle out away from the pipe cleaners.
4. Fold back a matching section of the second circle.
5. Have an adult help staple the circles together with the pipe cleaners between them. Do not staple the folded sections.
6. Bend the ends of pipe cleaners to resemble spider legs.
7. Attach the circles to the balloon by taping the folded sections to the balloon to make the two parts of a spider's body.
8. Draw eight eyes with the chalk.
9. Let the spiderling balloon from the ceiling using the string.

Questions

1. What is an egg sac made of? (silk from the mother spider)
2. What are baby spiders called? (spiderlings)
3. What part of the spider's body makes the silk? (the spinnerets)
4. How do spiderlings travel to new places? (by ballooning)
5. Describe how spiderlings go ballooning. (They release silk and the breeze picks the silk threads up and carries the spiderlings.)

www.harcourtschoolsupply.com
© Harcourt Achieve Inc. All rights reserved.

Science Activities
Arts and Crafts Across the Curriculum 1, SV 1419023543

GORGEOUS GEODES

Science Standard
Observes and describes
differences in rocks

Vocabulary
rocks
minerals
crystals
geodes
hollow

Discussion

- Rocks are made of one or more minerals. These minerals vary in color and texture.
- A geode is a spherical lump with a hollow cavity filled with crystals.
- The exterior of a geode is generally limestone while the interior is quartz crystals.
- The size, form, and shade of color of the crystals can vary greatly, making each geode unique.
- The inside of a geode is a surprise until it is cut or broken open.

www.harcourtschoolsupply.com
© Harcourt Achieve Inc. All rights reserved.

Science Activities
Arts and Crafts Across the Curriculum 1, SV 1419023543

Materials

- a geode
- one pantyhose plastic egg or small plastic egg per student
- brown lunch sacks
- iridescent glitter
- purple, gold, and silver glitter
- box lid or bowl
- glue
- scissors

Directions

Teacher Preparation

1. Display a geode and discuss how it is made.
2. Cut the lunch sacks along one side and cut off the bottom. If students are using the smaller eggs, cut the sacks into thirds.

Student Directions

1. Get a cut sack and crush it into a ball. Open it up and flatten it out.
2. Get half of a plastic egg and cover the outside with a layer of glue.
3. Wrap the sack around the outside of the egg to form the outside of the geode. The sack does not have to be smooth.
4. Spread glue inside the egg and push the edges of the sack over the edge of the egg. The glue will hold the edges of the sack in place.
5. Sprinkle glitter inside the egg. Shake the excess glitter into a box lid or bowl.
6. Set the geode aside to dry.

Questions

1. What are rocks made of? (minerals)
2. How is the inside of a geode different from most other rocks? (It is hollow inside.)
3. What kind of minerals are inside a geode? (crystals)
4. What shape is a geode? (a sphere)
5. What makes geodes unique? (the size, form and color of the crystals inside the geode)

www.harcourtschoolsupply.com
© Harcourt Achieve Inc. All rights reserved.

FEATHERY BIRDS

Vocabulary
birds
feathers
wings
flight
camouflage

Discussion

- All birds have feathers, and they are the only animals that have them.
- Birds have soft, downy feathers close to their bodies that help keep them warm.
- They have strong wing and tail feathers that allow for flight. All of the feathers are lightweight
- The color of a bird's feathers helps camouflage them from predators or helps them attract a mate. Most male birds have brighter colored feathers than female birds.
- Although all birds have wings and feathers, not all birds can fly, such as penguins and ostriches.

www.harcourtschoolsupply.com
© Harcourt Achieve Inc. All rights reserved.

Materials

- patterns on page 90
- various colors of construction paper
- yellow or orange construction paper
- craft feathers in a variety of colors
- wiggly eyes
- old file folders
- tape
- scissors
- glue
- pencils

Directions

Teacher Preparation

Duplicate the egg, wing, tail, foot, and beak patterns on file folders to use as templates. Enlarge patterns if desired. Cut out the patterns.

Student Directions

1. Trace and cut out the egg, tail, and wing patterns on the desired color of construction paper.
2. Trace and cut out the beak and two feet patterns from yellow or orange construction paper.
3. Glue one wiggly eye on the small end of the egg.
4. Glue the beak on the same end of the egg.
5. Glue the tail on the large end of the egg opposite the beak.
6. Glue the two legs on the bottom side of the egg.
7. Glue the wing in the middle of the egg.
8. Tape one or two craft feathers on the wing.
9. Look at each feather and decide if it is a soft, downy feather or a strong, flight feather.

Questions

1. What does a bird have that no other animal has? (feathers)
2. Are a bird's feathers all the same? (No, some are soft to keep them warm and some are strong to help them fly.)
3. Do most male or female birds have brighter colored feathers? (male)
4. How can the color of a bird's feathers help protect it from predators? (The color blends in with the environment around the bird.)
5. Name two birds that cannot fly. (penguin and ostrich)

www.harcourtschoolsupply.com
© Harcourt Achieve Inc. All rights reserved.

Science Activities
Arts and Crafts Across the Curriculum 1, SV 1419023543

TUBE THERMOMETER

Science Standard
Observes and records
changes in the weather

Vocabulary
temperature
thermometer
mercury
degrees
Fahrenheit
Celsius

Discussion

- Air temperature is measured by a mercury thermometer, which uses the principle of contraction and expansion.
- When the temperature rises, the mercury expands and rises in the thermometer tube.
- Cold weather makes the mercury contract and fall in the thermometer tube.
- On the Fahrenheit scale, which is used in the United States, 32° is the freezing point of water.
- The Celsius, or centigrade scale, is used by the World Meteorological Organization and most countries in the world. On this scale, 0° is the freezing point.

Questions

1. What tool is used to measure the air temperature? (a thermometer)
2. What happens to the mercury in a thermometer when the air is hot? (It expands and goes up.)
3. What does cold air do to the mercury in a thermometer? (It makes it contract and go down.)
4. What is the freezing point on the Fahrenheit scale? (32°)

www.harcourtschoolsupply.com
© Harcourt Achieve Inc. All rights reserved.

Science Activities
Arts and Crafts Across the Curriculum 1, SV 1419023543

Materials

- a thermometer
- one paper towel tube per student
- white copy paper
- $\frac{1}{2}$-inch wide elastic
- red markers
- ruler
- craft sticks
- stapler
- retractable utility knife
- pencil or pen
- scissors
- glue

Directions

Teacher Preparation

1. Use a ruler to mark off fourteen half-inch spaces in the center of a sheet of copy paper.
2. Write a *0* to the left of the third mark from the bottom. This will be the 0° mark on the thermometer.
3. Duplicate the thermometer lines for each student.
4. Cut the white paper to fit the circumference of the paper towel tube.
5. When students have covered their tube, cut a slit at the top and the bottom of the tube slightly to the right of the numbers.
6. Cut an 18-inch section of elastic for each student.
7. Staple a craft stick on one end of the elastic.
8. When students have completed their thermometer, staple a craft stick to the free end of the elastic. This will allow the elastic to be moved without coming out of the slits.

Student Directions

1. Starting at 0 on the white paper, go up and count by tens to 110. Write the correct number by each line on the thermometer.
2. Going down from 0, count by tens to 20. Write a number by each line.
3. Spread a thin layer of glue over the tube.
4. Cover the tube with the white paper, making sure the paper is smooth.
5. Have an adult cut a slit at each end of the tube slightly to the right of the numbers.
6. Color about eight inches of the elastic red starting at the end with the craft stick.
7. Push the free end of the elastic out through the slit at the bottom of the tube.
8. Push the end of the elastic in through the slit at the top. Reach inside the tube and continue pulling the elastic out of the top of the tube.
9. Have an adult staple a craft stick to the free end of elastic.
10. Look at the class thermometer each day and move the elastic to record the correct temperature.

www.harcourtschoolsupply.com
© Harcourt Achieve Inc. All rights reserved.

Science Activities
Arts and Crafts Across the Curriculum 1, SV 1419023543

ROTATING EARTH

Science Standard
Observes, describes, and
records changes in position

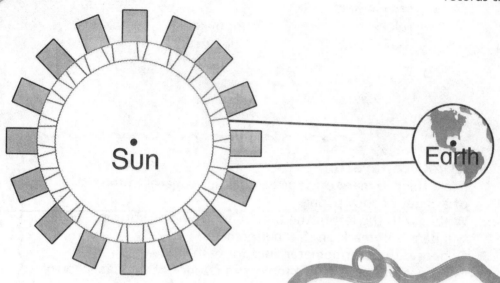

Vocabulary

Earth
sun
star
rotate
revolve

Discussion

- The sun is a star which is a burning ball of gas.
- The sun is the closest star to Earth and provides it with heat and light.
- Earth rotates on its axis and revolves around the sun at the same time.
- It takes Earth 24 hours or one day to complete one rotation.
- It takes Earth 365 days or one year to revolve around the sun one time.

Materials

- one paper plate per student
- blue poster board
- white, yellow, and orange construction paper
- baby food jar lids for templates
- paper cutter
- cups of water

- one-inch brads
- watercolor paints
- paint shirts or aprons
- paintbrushes
- hole punch

- pencil
- crayons
- scissors
- glue

Directions

Teacher Preparation

1. Use the paper cutter to cut poster board into one-by-twelve-inch strips. Provide one strip per student.
2. Punch at hole at each end of the poster board strips.
3. Use a pencil to poke a hole in the center of the paper plates.
4. Cut yellow and orange construction paper into one-by-three-inch strips.

Student Directions

1. Use the watercolors to paint the bottom of the paper plate yellow. Set it aside to dry.
2. Trace the baby food jar lid to make a circle on the white construction paper and cut it out.
3. Color the circle to resemble the planet Earth including oceans, land, and clouds. Write *Earth* on the planet.
4. Punch a hole in the center of the Earth.
5. Attach the Earth to one end of the poster board strip by putting a brad through the holes.
6. Glue yellow and orange strips of paper around the edge of the plate for the rays of the sun.
7. Attach the paper plate sun to the other end of the poster board strip using a brad. Write *Sun* on the plate.
8. Move the pieces to show how Earth rotates and revolves around the sun at the same time.

Questions

1. What is the sun made of? (It is a star that is made of burning gas.)
2. How does the sun help Earth? (It provides Earth with heat and light.)
3. How long does it take Earth to rotate one time? (24 hours or one day)
4. How long does it take Earth to revolve around the sun? (365 days or one year)

www.harcourtschoolsupply.com
© Harcourt Achieve Inc. All rights reserved.

Science Activities
Arts and Crafts Across the Curriculum 1, SV 1419023543

FROG ON A LOG

Science Standard
Identifies basic needs
of living organisms

Vocabulary

frog

amphibian

tadpole

tongue

hibernate

Discussion

- Amphibians, which include frogs, are animals that spend the first part of their life cycle in the water and the adult part mostly on land.
- Frogs breathe through gills as tadpoles or babies and through lungs as adults.
- While frogs are hibernating in the winter, they also breathe through their skin.
- Frogs live on land as adults but must live near water to keep their skin moist to avoid dehydration.
- Their skin absorbs water into their body so they do not have to drink water to survive.
- Most frogs have a sticky tongue that they can flip out to catch an insect.

www.harcourtschoolsupply.com
© Harcourt Achieve Inc. All rights reserved.

Science Activities
Arts and Crafts Across the Curriculum 1, SV 1419023543

Materials

- patterns on page 91
- one paper towel tube per student
- two paper plates per student
- green and red construction paper
- green and red tempera paint
- paintbrushes
- writing paper
- paint shirts or aprons
- pencils
- markers
- scissors
- glue

Directions

Teacher Preparation

1. Duplicate on green construction paper two arms, two legs, and two eyes for each student.
2. Set up a paint station with green and red paint.

Student Directions

1. Paint the bottom of one paper plate green. Set it aside to dry.
2. Paint the top of a second paper plate red. Set it aside to dry.
3. Glue the paper plates together with the red on top.
4. Fold the paper plates in half to make the mouth of the frog.
5. Cut out the arms, legs, and eyes.
6. Glue the arms on the side of the mouth and the legs on the bottom of the mouth.
7. Use a black marker to draw the center of the eyes.
8. Fold a small section on the straight side of the eyes. Place glue on the folded sections of the eyes and glue them on the outside fold of the paper plate so that they stand up.
9. Cut a long, thin piece of red construction paper for the tongue. Roll it around a pencil to curl it and glue it inside the mouth.
10. Glue the frog on a paper towel tube for the log.
11. Write or dictate a sentence on writing paper that tells about frogs. Put the sentence inside the log.

Questions

1. What kind of animal is a frog? (an amphibian)
2. What is unique about the life cycle of an amphibian? (It spends part of its life in the water and part on land.)
3. How do tadpoles breathe? (through gills) adult frogs breathe? (lungs)
4. How do frogs breathe while they are hibernating? (through their skin)
5. Do frogs drink water? (No, they absorb water through their skin.)

www.harcourtschoolsupply.com
© Harcourt Achieve Inc. All rights reserved.

Science Activities
Arts and Crafts Across the Curriculum 1, SV 1419023543

OWL PUPPET

Science Standard
Identifies characteristics of living organisms

Vocabulary

bird

owl

prey

nocturnal

pellets

Discussion

- Owls are birds of prey that have large heads, flat faces, forward-directed eyes, hooked beaks, strong legs, sharp claws, and soft feathers.
- Most owls are nocturnal, which means they sleep during the day and hunt for food at night.
- Most owls have excellent eyesight. Their eyes do not move in their sockets so they have to move their entire head to look around.
- Owls have soft feathers so they can sneak up on their prey silently.
- Owls eat smaller prey whole and larger prey in chunks. They cough up parts that cannot be digested such as hair, fur, and bones in oval-shaped pellets.

www.harcourtschoolsupply.com
© Harcourt Achieve Inc. All rights reserved.

Science Activities
Arts and Crafts Across the Curriculum 1, SV 1419023543

Materials

- patterns on page 92
- one brown lunch sack per student
- brown, black, and yellow construction paper
- brown pipe cleaners
- a $2\frac{1}{2}$-inch lid
- a 2-inch lid
- old file folders
- scissors
- glue
- pencils

Directions

Teacher Preparation
Duplicate and trace the wing, beak, and tuft patterns on file folders to use as templates.

Student Directions
1. Trace and cut out two wings and a tuft on brown construction paper.
2. Turn a lunch sack upside down and glue the tuft pattern on the bottom flap of the sack and the wings on the side.
3. Trace the larger lid twice on yellow construction paper.
4. Cut them out and glue them on the bottom flap of the lunch sack so that they overlap the tuft.
5. Trace the smaller lid twice on black construction paper.
6. Cut them out and glue them on top of the yellow circles to make the pupils of the eyes.
7. Trace and cut out the beak on yellow construction paper.
8. Glue it below the eyes.
9. Cut and bend two short pieces of brown pipe cleaners for each of the owl's legs and talons.
10. Poke them through the lower edge of the lunch sack and twist the ends to secure them to the sack.

Questions

1. Name two characteristics of an owl. (Answers will vary.)
2. What does nocturnal mean? (sleeps during the day and looks for food at night)
3. How are an owl's eyes different from the eyes of other birds? (Their eyes do not move, and they have to turn their whole head to look around.)
4. What is special about an owl's feathers that allows it to sneak up on its prey? (The owl's feathers are soft and make no sound.)
5. What is an owl pellet? (It is the fur, hair, and bones that an owl coughs up.)

49

www.harcourtschoolsupply.com
© Harcourt Achieve Inc. All rights reserved.

THREE-PART SEED

Science Standard
Observes and describes
the parts of plants

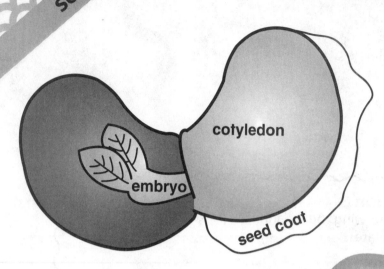

Vocabulary

seeds
embryo
cotyledon
seed coat
leaves
root

Discussion

- All seeds need water, oxygen, and proper temperature to germinate or start growing.
- Inside the seed is a tiny, baby plant that is called the embryo.
- The embryo consists of a root and a stem and leaves called a shoot.
- The cotyledon provides the embryo with food until the root and leaves get started feeding the plant.
- The protective outer covering of a seed is called the seed coat.

© Harcourt Achieve Inc. All rights reserved.
Arts and Crafts Across the Curriculum 1, SV 1419023543

Materials

- patterns on page 93
- lima beans soaked in water
- white and green construction paper
- waxed paper
- magnifying glass
- pencils
- black permanent writing marker
- old file folders

- stapler
- scissors
- glue

Directions

Teacher Preparation

1. Duplicate the seed and embryo and trace them on old file folders for use as templates.
2. Use a permanent black marker to trace the seed template on the waxed paper. Provide one for each student.
3. When students have completed their seed, help them staple the pieces together.

Student Directions

1. Look at a lima bean seed and remove the seed coat.
2. Open the cotyledon and look through a magnifying glass at the embryo.
3. Trace the seed template on a folded sheet of white construction paper.
4. Cut out the seed on the folded paper to get two seeds that match. These are the cotyledon.
5. Cut out the seed coat from the waxed paper.
6. Trace the embryo template on green construction paper and cut it out.
7. Layer the seed pieces together with the embryo between the two halves of the seed and the seed coat on top.
8. Have an adult help staple the pieces together on one end.
9. Write the words *seed coat*, *cotyledon*, and *embryo* on the correct parts of the seed.

Questions

1. What does a seed need to start growing? (water, oxygen, and the right temperature)
2. What and where is the embryo of a seed? (a tiny, baby plant inside the seed)
3. What is the cotyledon part of the seed? (a temporary food supply that is around the baby plant)
4. What is the thin, outside covering of the seed called? (the seed coat)
5. What is the function of the seed coat? (to protect the embryo or baby plant)

www.harcourtschoolsupply.com
© Harcourt Achieve Inc. All rights reserved.

Science Activities
Arts and Crafts Across the Curriculum 1, SV 1419023543

FOOD PYRAMID MOBILE

Science Standard
Identifies basic food groups

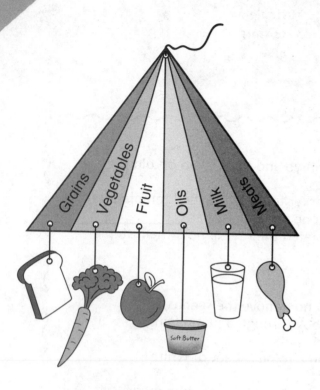

Vocabulary
grains
Food Guide Pyramid
vegetables
fruits
meat and beans
milk
oils

Discussion

- The Food Guide Pyramid has been updated to help in the choosing of healthy foods along with the recommended amounts of foods per serving.
- The Food Guide Pyramid consists of six sections which include grains, vegetables, fruits, meats and beans, milk, and oils.
- It recommends whole grains, low-fat meats and milk, and oils with no trans fatty acids.
- Daily exercise is also a part of the new Food Guide Pyramid.
- The website mypyramid.gov offers a plan for each individual according to his or her age, sex, and activity level.

Materials

- Food Pyramid Poster
- white poster board
- old magazines with food pictures
- ruler
- hole punch
- yarn
- markers
- scissors
- construction paper
- glue

Directions

Teacher Preparation

1. Use the ruler to draw an equilateral triangle with twelve-inch sides on the poster board. Cut them out and provide one for each student.
2. Use the ruler to divide the triangles into six equal sections.
3. Cut the yarn into six-inch pieces. Provide seven pieces for each student.
4. Discuss with students the Food Guide Pyramid. Display the poster.

Student Directions

1. Color the sections on the triangle to match the Food Pyramid.
2. Punch a hole at the top of the triangle.
3. Tie a piece of yarn through the hole.
4. Punch a hole at the bottom of each section of the triangle.
5. Tie a piece of yarn through each hole.
6. Cut out a picture from a magazine of a food from each of the six food groups on the Food Pyramid.
7. Glue the pictures on construction paper to make them sturdier.
8. Cut around the pictures so that the shape of the construction paper matches each picture.
9. Punch a hole at the top of each picture.
10. Tie the free end of the yarn of each section to the picture that belongs in that food group.
11. Write the name of each food group in the appropriate section of the triangle.
12. Hang the mobile if desired.

Questions

1. What is the Food Guide Pyramid for? (It helps people choose foods that are healthy.)
2. How many food groups are on the Food Guide Pyramid? (six)
3. Besides eating good foods, what else does the Food Guide Pyramid suggest people do to stay healthy? (exercise)

Science

www.harcourtschoolsupply.com
© Harcourt Achieve Inc. All rights reserved.

Science Activities
Arts and Crafts Across the Curriculum 1, SV 1419023543

INSECT HOTELS

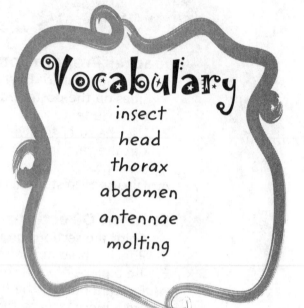

Vocabulary

insect
head
thorax
abdomen
antennae
molting

Discussion

- Insects have three main body parts which are a head, thorax, and an abdomen.
- They have six jointed legs and two antennae for sensing things around them.
- Insects have an outside, protective shell that is called an exoskeleton.
- Many insects molt or shed their outer skeleton and replace it with a larger one as they grow.
- Most insects have one or two pairs of wings for flying.

© Harcourt Achieve Inc. All rights reserved.

Materials

- one oatmeal box with lid per student
- paint
- paintbrushes
- paint shirts or aprons
- netting or wire screen
- insect stickers
- markers
- scissors
- magnifying glasses
- drawing paper
- plastic tape

Directions

Teacher Preparation

1. Cut out a large window on the side of the each oatmeal box.
2. Cut a piece of netting or wire screen slightly larger than the window.
3. Attach the netting or wire screen securely on the window with plastic tape.

Student Directions

1. Paint the oatmeal box and lid with the desired color of paint and set it aside to dry.
2. Decorate the box with markers and stickers.
3. Go outside to search for and catch an insect. Be sure to provide your "tenant" with food and water.
4. Use a magnifying glass to observe the insect.
5. Draw a picture showing the parts of an insect's body.

Questions

1. Name the three body parts of an insect. (head, thorax, abdomen)
2. How many legs does an insect have? (six)
3. What are the antennae used for? (to sense things around the insect)
4. What is an exoskeleton? (a protective outer shell)
5. How do insects molt? (They shed their outer shell when they outgrow it and replace it with a larger one.)

www.harcourtschoolsupply.com
© Harcourt Achieve Inc. All rights reserved.

PLASTER FOSSILS

Science Standard
Understands the properties
of earth materials

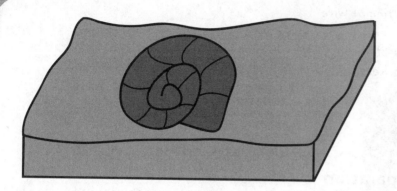

Vocabulary

fossils
sedimentary
layers
cast
mold

Discussion

- Fossils are the remains of plants or animals or other artifacts such as footprints that have turned to stone.
- Fossils are formed when the minerals in an object are replaced by other minerals.
- Fossils are most often found in sedimentary rock, which is formed by layers of minerals.
- Mold fossils are the fossilized impressions that leave the shape of plants or animals.
- Cast fossils are those that are formed when a mold is filled in.

Materials

- one half-pint milk carton per student
- plaster of Paris
- modeling clay
- large butter tub
- old spoon
- water
- small objects such as shells or small plastic dinosaurs
- toothpicks
- scissors

Directions

Teacher Preparation

1. Thoroughly rinse the milk cartons and allow them to dry.
2. Cut off the top half of each milk carton and throw it away.
3. When students have the molds ready, mix a batch of plaster of Paris in the butter tub according to package directions. Because the plaster will begin to harden fairly quickly, it is best not to mix up too much at one time.

Student Directions

1. Pinch off a piece of clay the size of the bottom of the milk carton.
2. Press the clay into the milk carton covering all of the corners. The clay should be about one inch thick.
3. Select an object such as a shell or small dinosaur that will fit into the milk carton.
4. Lay the object on its side and press it firmly into the clay.
5. Gently remove the object so that the imprint is visible.
6. Have an adult prepare the plaster of Paris and then cover the imprint with a layer of the plaster about a half-inch thick.
7. Use a toothpick to write your initials in the plaster after allowing it to set for a minute or two.
8. Let the plaster harden overnight.
9. Tear away the milk carton and dispose of it properly.
10. Gently pull the plaster away from the clay to reveal a cast and a mold "fossil" of the object that was used to make the imprint.

Questions

1. What are the remains of plants and animals that have turned to stone called? (fossils)
2. What kind of rocks are most fossils found in? (sedimentary rocks)
3. How are sedimentary rocks formed? (by layers)
4. Describe a mold fossil. (an impression that leaves the shape of a plant or animal)
5. What is a fossil called that is formed when a mold fossil is filled in? (cast)

57

SEA HORSE FAMILY

Science Standard
Observes the life
cycle of organisms

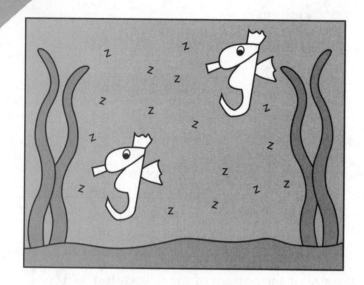

Vocabulary

sea horse

pouch

eggs

life cycle

hatch

Discussion

- Even though a sea horse has a head shaped like a horse and a monkey-like tail. A sea horse is really a fish.
- Sea horses can change color to blend in with their surroundings as a means of protection.
- The female sea horse lays several hundred eggs at a time.
- The male sea horse has a pouch on the front of his body in which the female deposits her eggs.
- The father carries them for 2–3 weeks until they hatch.
- Like all fish, sea horses do not take care of their babies after they are hatched. About five out of a thousand babies survive.

www.harcourtschoolsupply.com
© Harcourt Achieve Inc. All rights reserved.

Science Activities
Arts and Crafts Across the Curriculum 1, SV 1419023543

Materials

- white construction paper
- blue watercolor paint or thinned tempera paint
- paintbrushes
- pencils
- crayons
- paint shirts or aprons

Directions

Teacher Preparation

Prepare a paint center for blue paint.

Student Directions

1. Use crayons to draw sand across the bottom of a sheet of white construction paper.
2. Draw some seaweed with a green crayon on both sides of the paper. Press hard with the crayon.
3. Use a pencil to draw a father and a mother sea horse by writing a large lowercase *g*.
4. The top of the *g* will be the head of the sea horse. Draw a snout and an eye.
5. On the hook part of the *g* below the head, draw a belly and the monkey-like tail.
6. Draw a fin on the back and on the head of the sea horses.
7. Press hard with crayons to color the sea horses.
8. Draw several tiny letter *Z*s with a black crayon to make baby sea horses. Press hard on the crayon.
9. Paint a blue wash across the entire picture to resemble the ocean.

Questions

1. What kind of animal is a sea horse? (a fish)
2. How do sea horses protect themselves? (by changing their color to blend in with their surroundings)
3. About how many eggs does the mother sea horse lay? (several hundred)
4. Where does the mother deposit her eggs? (in the father's pouch)
5. Do the mother and father sea horses take care of their babies once they hatch? (No, they are on their own.)

www.harcourtschoolsupply.com
© Harcourt Achieve Inc. All rights reserved.

Science Activities
Arts and Crafts Across the Curriculum 1, SV 1419023543

LINCOLN'S LOG CABIN

Social Studies Standard

Identifies the contributions of historical figures that helped to shape our nation

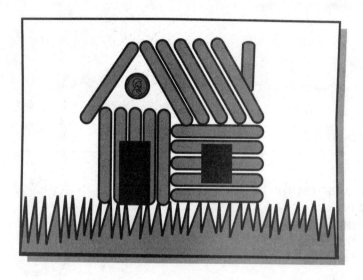

Vocabulary

Abraham Lincoln
president
log cabin
Civil War
slavery

Discussion

- Abraham Lincoln was born in a log cabin in Kentucky on February 12, 1809.
- As a boy, Lincoln lived a humble life as the son of a farmer.
- He later became a lawyer and was elected the sixteenth president of the United States in 1860.
- Lincoln is remembered as one of the great presidents for his role in preserving the Union during the Civil War.
- He was responsible for beginning the process that led to the end of slavery in the United States.

Materials

- white, brown, and green construction paper
- 17–18 jumbo craft sticks per student
- one Lincoln penny per student
- brown tempera paint
- paintbrushes
- paint shirts or aprons
- scissors
- glue

Directions

Teacher Preparation

1. Cut green construction paper into two-inch-by-twelve-inch strips.
2. Cut the brown construction paper into fourths.
3. Set up a paint station with brown paint.

Student Directions

1. Paint one side of the craft sticks brown and set them aside to dry.
2. Use the scissors to fringe the green construction paper strips to resemble grass.
3. Glue the grass to the longer edge of a full sheet of white construction paper.
4. Lay jumbo craft sticks above the grass to form a log cabin. Glue five sticks vertically for the front of the cabin and five sticks horizontally for the side of the cabin.
5. Glue five diagonally above the horizontal sticks to form the roof and one above the front of the house to form the point on the roof.
6. Break one stick in half for the chimney and glue it on the house.
7. Cut a window and a door from the brown construction paper.
8. Glue the door on the vertical sticks and the window on the horizontal sticks.
9. Glue a Lincoln penny in the triangular space above the door.

Questions

1. Where and when was Abraham Lincoln born? (in Kentucky on February 12, 1809)
2. What kind of house did he grow up in? (a log cabin)
3. What kind of job did he have before he became president? (a lawyer)
4. In what year was Lincoln elected president? (1860)
5. For what is Lincoln most remembered for doing while he was president? (stopping slavery)

www.harcourtschoolsupply.com
© Harcourt Achieve Inc. All rights reserved.

Social Studies Activities
Arts and Crafts Across the Curriculum 1, SV 1419023543

FAMOUS LEADER MASKS

Social Studies Standard
Identifies leaders in the community, state, and nation

Vocabulary
government
president
vice president
governor
mayor

Discussion

- The president of United States can be elected as the chief officer of the executive branch of the government.
- The president is elected to serve a four-year term and can serve a maximum of two terms.
- The vice president of the United States can be given the power to assume the duties of the president under conditions of absence, illness, or death.
- Each of the fifty states elects a governor as the highest office of authority for that state.
- A mayor is elected as the head government official for a town or city.

Materials

- pictures of local, state, or national leaders from books or newspapers
- one paper plate per student
- jumbo craft sticks
- construction paper
- yarn of various hair colors
- crayons or markers
- scissors
- glue
- tape

Directions

Teacher Preparation

Cut out two circles from the center of the paper plates for eyes of the mask.

Student Directions

1. Find a picture of a local, state, or national leader. Make a mask of this person.
2. Use markers to draw eyelashes and eyebrows around the eye cutouts.
3. Use markers to draw a nose and mouth on the plate.
4. Cut strips of construction paper or pieces of yarn for the person's hair.
5. Glue the hair on the mask.
6. Add other details such as earrings, eyeglasses, a moustache, or beard if appropriate.
7. Tape a craft stick on the back of the plate for a handle.
8. Learn and tell something about the leader.

Questions

1. Name the President of the United States. (Answer will be the current president.)
2. Who does the job of the president if for some reason the president cannot do it? (the vice-president)
3. Who is the leader of each state? (the governor)
4. Who is the leader of each town or city? (the mayor)
5. Name one thing that a leader of a city, state, or nation might do at their job. (Answers will vary.)

www.harcourtschoolsupply.com
© Harcourt Achieve Inc. All rights reserved.

SOAPBOX TOWN

Social Studies Standard
Identifies places to acquire basic goods and services

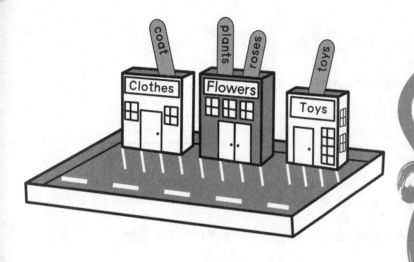

Vocabulary

goods
services
businesses
buy
sell

Discussion

- Goods are defined as things that people want or need.
- Services are duties or work that is done to help people.
- Businesses earn money by selling goods and/or services.
- The payment for goods and services is made by individuals.
- Services such as those provided by firefighters or police officers are paid for by tax money that is collected from the public.

Materials

- three or four empty boxes from bar soap or juice boxes per student
- one shoe box lid per student
- construction paper
- yellow paint
- small paintbrushes
- craft sticks
- scissors
- markers or crayons
- paint shirts or aprons
- glue

Directions

Teacher Preparation

1. Cut construction paper to fit the soap or juice box.
2. Cut off the flaps on one end of each soap or juice box.
3. Discuss with students the goods and services people get from different stores.

Student Directions

1. Glue construction paper around each box.
2. Draw a door and windows on each box to resemble a store.
3. Make a sign for each store that tells what the store sells.
4. Glue the bottom of the stores inside the shoe box lid so that they are up against the side of the lid.
5. Paint yellow parking stripes by the stores on the lid and traffic lines down the middle of the "street."
6. Write the name on a craft stick of a good or a service that might be sold in each store, such as coats in a clothing store.
7. Place the sticks inside the box of the correct store.

Questions

1. What are goods? (things that people need or want)
2. What are services? (duties or work done to help people)
3. Who pays for the services of firefighters? (the tax money that is collected from the people of the community)
4. How do businesses earn money? (by selling goods and services)
5. What kind of goods would be sold at a florist? (flowers or plants)

www.harcourtschoolsupply.com
© Harcourt Achieve Inc. All rights reserved.

FOURTH OF JULY WINDSOCK

Social Studies Standard
Identifies customs associated with national patriotic holidays

Vocabulary
Independence Day
Fourth of July
holiday
parade
fireworks

Discussion

- Independence Day is also known as the Fourth of July and the birthday of the United States of America.
- The Fourth of July is a holiday or a day off from work for people to celebrate the adoption of the *Declaration of Independence* on July 4, 1776.
- The Fourth of July was set aside as a national holiday in 1941.
- The day was originally celebrated in 1776 with a parade and cannon fire. The tradition of parades on Independence Day is continued today.
- Fireworks take the place of cannon fire today.

© Harcourt Achieve Inc. All rights reserved.

Materials

- one white lunch sack per student
- red and blue crepe paper streamers
- red or blue yarn
- red and blue markers or crayons
- white glitter
- hole punch
- scissors
- glue

Directions

Teacher Preparation

1. Cut off the bottom end of the lunch sacks.
2. Fold the top edge of the lunch sacks over twice to reinforce the end.

Student Directions

1. Punch a hole on each side of the folded end of the sack.
2. Tie each end of a piece of yarn through the two holes in the sack for the handle.
3. Color all sides of the folded edge of the sack blue.
4. Color red vertical stripes around the sack.
5. Cut two-foot red and blue streamers.
6. Glue the streamers to the inside edge of the sack.
7. Add dots of white glitter on the blue fold.
8. Take the windsock outside and hold it high to let the wind blow through it.

Questions

1. Why is Independence Day celebrated? (It is the birthday of the United States.)
2. On what date is Independence Day celebrated? (July 4th)
3. What was different about Independence Day when it was made a national holiday? (People got a day off from work to celebrate.)
4. Describe what might be seen in a Fourth of July parade. (Answers will vary.)
5. What is used today to celebrate Independence Day instead of cannon fire? (fireworks)

67

© Harcourt Achieve Inc. All rights reserved.

SALT DOUGH MAP

Social Studies Standard
Identifies Earth's features
on maps, such as rivers,
oceans, and mountains

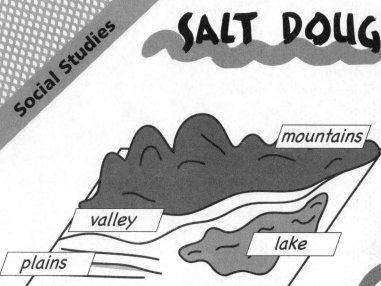

Vocabulary

Earth
map
valleys
mountains
rivers

Discussion

- Three-fourths of the planet Earth is covered by bodies of water.
- About 97% of Earth's water is the salt water in the oceans, and 3% is fresh water.
- There are over 20 major rivers that cross the North American continent and over 800 smaller branches or tributaries.
- Landforms include continents, ocean basins, plains, plateaus, and mountain ranges.
- A valley is a low place between hills or mountains.
- A mountain is a landform that is higher than the surrounding land, and it is higher and steeper than a hill.

www.harcourtschoolsupply.com
© Harcourt Achieve Inc. All rights reserved.

Materials

- one five-inch square of cardboard per student
- flour
- salt
- water
- bowl
- blue and brown tempera paint
- spoon
- measuring cups
- paint shirts or aprons
- index cards

- paintbrushes
- pencils
- scissors
- tape

Directions

Teacher Preparation

1. Mix together 2 cups flour and 1 cup salt and then add water until the consistency of dough. Knead the dough until smooth. Increase the recipe as needed and provide each student with a two-inch ball of dough.
2. Set up a paint center with blue and brown paint.

Student Directions

1. Press the dough onto the cardboard. Leave a narrow border around the edge of the cardboard.
2. Use fingers to shape the dough into various landforms such as mountains, a valley, plains, and a river or lake.
3. Let the dough dry overnight.
4. Paint the water areas blue.
5. Paint the land areas brown.
6. Cut an index card to make labels for each landform.
7. Write the name of each landform on a label.
8. Tape the labels around the edge of the map.

Questions

1. Is the Earth covered with more land or water areas? (water)
2. What kind of water is found in rivers? (fresh water)
3. Name a landform. (Answers will vary.)
4. Where is a valley located? (in a low area between hills or mountains)
5. Is a hill or a mountain higher? (a mountain)

© Harcourt Achieve Inc. All rights reserved.
Arts and Crafts Across the Curriculum 1, SV 1419023543

THUMBPRINT FARM VS. CITY

Social Studies Standard
Compares and contrasts
a farm and a city

Cows live on a farm. | A city has buildings.

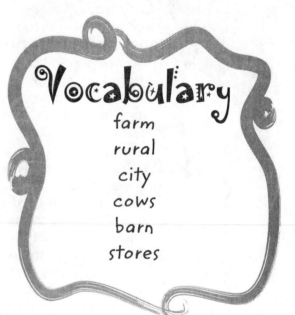

Vocabulary

farm
rural
city
cows
barn
stores

Discussion

- A rural area is a less populated area that is suitable for farming.
- A farm is a section of land that is used primarily for the production of food.
- Crops such as corn, potatoes, or beans may be grown on a farm for food.
- Animals such as cows, pigs, or chickens may be raised on a farm as a food source.
- A city is a more densely populated area where many businesses are located that provide goods and services for people.
- The food grown on a farm is often sold and transported to businesses in cities for people to consume.

www.harcourtschoolsupply.com
© Harcourt Achieve Inc. All rights reserved.

Social Studies Activities
Arts and Crafts Across the Curriculum 1, SV 1419023543

Materials

- pictures of a farm and of a city
- large white construction paper
- black ink pads
- crayons
- black fine-tip markers
- pencils

Directions

Teacher Preparation
Discuss with students the differences between a farm and a city.

Student Directions
1. Fold the white paper in half and draw a line down the crease with a black crayon.
2. On the left side of the paper, draw and color a farm scene. Include a barn and silo, a fence, and a large grassy area that is colored green.
3. Cover one thumb with black ink by pressing it on the ink pad.
4. Make a few thumbprint cows in the grassy area by pressing two thumbprints side by side. One thumbprint should be vertical for the head and the other one horizontal for the body.
5. Use the fine-tipped marker to draw ears, horns, eyes, legs, and a tail on each cow.
6. Write a sentence that tells about a farm across the top of the paper.
7. On the right side of the paper, draw and color a city scene that includes a few tall buildings, a street, and a car driving on the street.
8. Make thumbprint people in front of the buildings by pressing a few vertical thumbprints for the body.
9. Use the fine-tipped marker to draw face, hair, arms, and legs on the people.
10. Write a sentence that tells about a city across the top of the paper.

Questions

1. What is a farm used for? (to produce food)
2. What is one plant that is grown on a farm that provides food? (Answers will vary.)
3. What kind of animal that is raised on a farm provides people with eggs? (chickens)
4. Where does the food sold in grocery stores come from? (farms)
5. Describe how the buildings on a farm differ from the buildings in a city. (Answers will vary.)

www.harcourtschoolsupply.com
© Harcourt Achieve Inc. All rights reserved.

Social Studies Activities
Arts and Crafts Across the Curriculum 1, SV 1419023543

HAPPY EARTH NECKLACE

Social Studies Standard
Discusses ways people can take care of the environment

Vocabulary

environment
recycle
reuse
reduce
pollution
litter

Discussion

- Pollution is when human beings make the air, land, or water unclean. Noise pollution can also be a problem.
- People can lessen pollution by learning the three *R*s, which are reducing, reusing, and recycling.
- Using less paper and plastic are ways to reduce pollution.
- Reusing an item is finding a way to use it again without changing it. For example, plastic butter tubs can be used to store small objects.
- Recycling is when an item, such as newspapers, can be changed so that it can be used again as another item, such as writing paper.

www.harcourtschoolsupply.com
© Harcourt Achieve Inc. All rights reserved.

Social Studies Activities
Arts and Crafts Across the Curriculum 1, SV 1419023543

Materials

- modeling clay
- yarn or narrow ribbon
- markers
- an empty orange juice can for a shape cutter
- small rolling pin
- pencils
- scissors

Directions

Teacher Preparation

1. Discuss with students the importance of reducing, reusing, and recycling to help keep the environment clean.
2. Cut an 18-inch piece of yarn or ribbon for each student.
3. Help students tie the ends of the yarn or ribbon together, if necessary.

Student Directions

1. Roll out modeling clay to about one-quarter-inch thickness.
2. Use the open end of the juice can to cut out a circle of clay.
3. Make two holes with the pencil point about one inch apart close to the edge of the circle.
4. On one side of the circle, use a black marker to write *Keep Our Earth Clean*.
5. On the other side, color the circle to look like Earth.
6. Draw a happy face on Earth.
7. Thread a piece of yarn or ribbon through the two holes.
8. Tie the ends together to make a necklace.

Questions

1. Name three kinds of pollution. (air, land, water, or noise)
2. What are the three *R*s? (reduce, reuse, and recycle)
3. How can a plastic butter tub be reused? (Answers will vary.)
4. What is one item that can be recycled? (newspapers, plastic bottles, glass)

73

© Harcourt Achieve Inc. All rights reserved.

BUFFALO SKINS

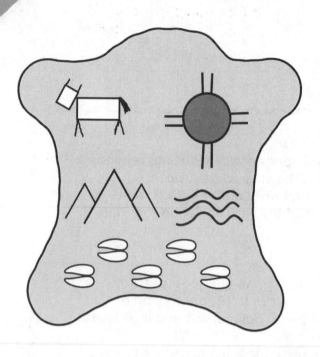

Vocabulary

Native Americans
buffalo
Plains
tepee
communicate

Discussion

- One of the most common ways that Native Americans used to communicate was the use of symbols which were picture drawings of objects done on rock walls, animal skins, or tree bark.
- Another form of communication was the use of sign language.
- Tribes could also communicate in a more simplistic way with the use of smoke or drum signals. This was usually done as a type of warning about possible danger.
- Most of the tribes of the Plains lived in tepees that were made from eight to twenty buffalo skins that were sewn together.
- They painted symbols or pictures on the skins using dyes made from various plants.

www.harcourtschoolsupply.com
© Harcourt Achieve Inc. All rights reserved.

Social Studies Activities
Arts and Crafts Across the Curriculum 1, SV 1419023543

Materials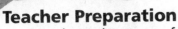

- pattern on page 94
- one brown grocery bag per student
- old poster board for use as a template
- overhead projector
- crayons or oil pastels
- scissors
- masking tape
- pencils

Directions

Teacher Preparation

1. Cut along the seam of the grocery bags and cut off the bottoms so that each bag lies flat.
2. Tape the poster board to the wall.
3. Use the overhead projector to enlarge the buffalo skin to the size of the grocery bag.
4. Cut out the buffalo skin for use as a template.
5. Demonstrate to students how to tear along the lines to give the buffalo skin a ragged edge.

Student Directions

1. Use the template to trace the buffalo skin on the plain side of the grocery bag.
2. Tear along the lines of the buffalo skin to give it a ragged edge.
3. Use crayons or oil pastels to draw symbols or pictures on the buffalo skin.
4. Tell a story using the symbols on the skin.

Questions

1. What is the most common way that Native Americans communicated with each other? (picture drawings or symbols)
2. Where might Native Americans draw pictures or symbols? (on rock walls, animal skins, or tree bark)
3. Why were smoke or drum signals used? (to warn others of danger)
4. How many buffalo skins did it take to make a tepee? (eight to twenty)
5. What did the Plains tribes use to paint symbols on their tepees? (dyes made from plants)

www.harcourtschoolsupply.com
© Harcourt Achieve Inc. All rights reserved.

NEW YEAR LANTERN

Social Studies Standard
Compares family customs and traditions

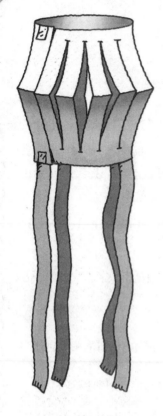

Vocabulary
Chinese New Year
celebration
tradition
lantern
legend

Discussion

- Preparation for the New Year in China begins by cleaning the house to sweep away bad luck and allow good luck to easily enter the home.
- The Chinese New Year celebrations last fifteen days. Each day has a special meaning and custom.
- At midnight on New Year's Eve, fireworks fill the sky in the belief that the colors and loud noises scare away evil spirits.
- The 15th day is called the Lantern Festival. Legend says that a god was angry with a town and threatened to destroy it with fire.
- People lit lanterns giving the appearance that the town was ablaze. The god left the town alone because he thought it was already on fire.

www.harcourtschoolsupply.com
© Harcourt Achieve Inc. All rights reserved.

Social Studies Activities
Arts and Crafts Across the Curriculum 1, SV 1419023543

Materials

- red construction paper
- red art supplies, such as sequins, stickers, and glitter
- red crepe paper streamers
- ruler
- tape
- stapler
- pencils
- scissors

Directions

Teacher Preparation

1. Draw a line one inch from the top along the length of the edge of the construction paper.
2. Help students staple the edges together to form a cylinder.

Student Directions

1. Hold the paper horizontally with the ruler line on the outside and fold the top and bottom edges together like a hot dog bun.
2. Draw vertical lines that are one inch apart from the pencil line to the folded edge.
3. Cut along the vertical lines.
4. Open the paper and fold it horizontally so the pencil marks are on the inside. Press the crease firmly.
5. Open the paper and use the art supplies to decorate the unmarked side.
6. Have an adult help staple the horizontal uncut edges together, forming a cylinder.
7. Cut streamers that are about three feet long.
8. Tape them to the bottom of the lantern.
9. Hang the lantern in the classroom.

Questions

1. Why do the Chinese clean their houses to prepare for the New Year? (to get rid of bad luck and let good luck in)
2. How many days does the Chinese New Year last? (fifteen)
3. What is the purpose of fireworks on New Year's Eve? (to scare away bad spirits)
4. What is the last day of the celebration called? (the Lantern Festival)
5. Why did the people light all the lanterns in town? (to trick a god into thinking the town was on fire)
6. Tell about one thing that your family does to celebrate New Year's Eve. (Answers will vary.)

JOHNNY APPLESEED STORY WHEEL

Social Studies Standard
Identifies ordinary people who helped shape the community

Legend of Johnny Appleseed

Vocabulary

Johnny Appleseed
John Chapman
pioneer
legend
orchards

Discussion

- John Chapman was an American pioneer who was born on September 26, 1774.
- Chapman traveled all through the Ohio Valley and sold or gave families apple seeds or saplings.
- He spent over 40 years helping settlers establish and care for apple orchards.
- His ragged dress and eccentric ways earned him the name of Johnny Appleseed.
- After his death, many stories were told about him in an exaggerated way. Thus began the legend of Johnny Appleseed.

www.harcourtschoolsupply.com
© Harcourt Achieve Inc. All rights reserved.

Materials

- pictures on page 95
- version of the story of Johnny Appleseed
- two paper plates per student
- one-inch brads
- ruler
- crayons
- scissors
- glue
- pencils

Directions

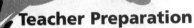

Teacher Preparation

1. Duplicate the story pictures for each student.
2. Find and mark the center point of a paper plate. Use a ruler to draw lines from the edge of the plate to the center point to mark off a quarter section of the plate.
3. Measure down three-inches from the edge on both lines. Use a ruler to connect the points.
4. Follow the lines and cut out the wedge.
5. Place the plate on top of a second plate and attach them at the center point with a brad to make a wheel.

Student Directions

1. Read the story about Johnny Appleseed.
2. Color and cut out the story pictures.
3. Glue the pictures in the correct sequence on the paper plate wheel, spacing them so that one picture shows at a time.
4. Write the title of the story across the front plate.
5. Turn the wheel and retell the story in sequence.

Questions

1. What was Johnny Appleseed's real name? (John Chapman)
2. When was John Chapman's birthday? (September 26, 1774)
3. What did he give or sell to families who were traveling west? (apple seeds or saplings)
4. What is a sapling? (a very small tree)
5. How did he spend the rest of his life? (helping settlers take care of the apple orchards)

www.harcourtschoolsupply.com
© Harcourt Achieve Inc. All rights reserved.

PAPER PLATE MAYFLOWER

Social Studies Standard
Discusses how various groups have gained or lost political freedom

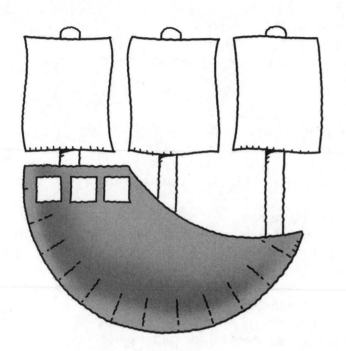

Vocabulary
Pilgrims
Mayflower
freedom
England
Thanksgiving

Discussion

- The Pilgrims sailed from England on the *Mayflower* on September 16, 1620.
- They left England in search of religious freedom.
- The *Mayflower* took 66 days to cross the Atlantic Ocean.
- Native Americans helped the Pilgrims survive the first year. The first Thanksgiving was a celebration of thanks.
- In 1863, Thanksgiving was declared a national holiday by President Abraham Lincoln on the last day in November. It was moved to the third Thursday in November in 1939.

© Harcourt Achieve Inc. All rights reserved.

Materials

- one small paper plate per student
- white construction paper
- crafts sticks
- ruler or measuring tape
- brown markers or crayons
- scissors
- glue

Directions

Teacher Preparation

1. Cut the white construction paper into three-inch strips.
2. Cut the paper plates in half.

Student Directions

1. Cut out a section of a paper plate so that it slopes like the front of the *Mayflower*.
2. Draw three small squares on the uncut part of the plate for ship windows.
3. Color the plate brown, but leave the windows white.
4. Cut a paper strip into three pieces to make sails.
5. Glue each paper sail on a craft stick.
6. Glue the sticks on the back of the paper plate ship.

Questions

1. What was the name of the ship that the Pilgrim's sailed on to America? (*Mayflower*)
2. From what country did the Pilgrims come? (England)
3. Why did they leave England? (for freedom of religion)
4. What do people do today to celebrate Thanksgiving? (get together with family, eat dinner, watch parades or football games)
5. Tell about something that you are thankful for. (Answers will vary.)

81

www.harcourtschoolsupply.com
© Harcourt Achieve Inc. All rights reserved.

UNCLE SAM STAND-UP DOLL

Social Studies Standard
Describes national patriotic symbols

Vocabulary
United States
Uncle Sam
nickname
top hat
goatee

Discussion

- Uncle Sam is a name used to represent the United States government and is thought to have originated during the War of 1812.
- Some sources attribute the name to Samuel Wilson (1766–1854), who was an inspector of army supplies. His nickname was "Uncle Sam."
- The "U.S." stamped on supplies was referred to as "Uncle Sam" by Samuel Wilson's workers.
- The first political drawing of Uncle Sam was done by Thomas Nast in the mid-1800s.
- Uncle Sam is usually drawn as a tall, elderly man with white hair and a goatee, a Stars and Stripes top hat; a red, white, and blue morning coat; and striped pants.

Questions

1. What name is used to represent the United States government? (Uncle Sam)
2. To whom was the nickname "Uncle Sam" first given? (Samuel Wilson)
3. What colors are Uncle Sam's clothes? (red, white, and blue like the colors in the United States flag)

www.harcourtschoolsupply.com
© Harcourt Achieve Inc. All rights reserved.

Social Studies Activities
Arts and Crafts Across the Curriculum 1, SV 1419023543

Materials

- one paper towel tube per student
- one four-ounce yogurt container per student (use the brand that has an edge so that it looks like a top hat when turned upside down)
- blue paint
- paintbrushes
- paint shirts or aprons
- dishwashing liquid
- pink, blue, and white construction paper
- cotton balls
- wiggly eyes
- gold glitter

- hot glue gun
- crayons or markers
- scissors
- glue

Directions

Teacher Preparation

1. Cut pink and blue construction paper into $2\frac{1}{2}$-by-6-inch strips. Provide one strip of each color per student.
2. Cut white construction paper into $3\frac{1}{2}$-by-6-inch strips. Provide one strip for each student.
3. Set up paint center with blue paint. Add a few drops of dishwashing liquid to the paint so that it will adhere to the plastic of the yogurt container.
4. When students have completed Uncle Sam, use hot glue to attach the "hat" on the top end of the tube.

Student Directions

1. Paint a blue band around the top of the yogurt container and vertical red stripes on the remaining part. Set it aside to dry.
2. Color red vertical stripes on the white construction paper to make Uncle Sam's pants.
3. Spread a thin layer of glue on the back of the white paper and wrap it around the bottom end of the paper towel tube.
4. Repeat step 3 with the blue paper for the jacket and place it above the "pants."
5. Squeeze three dots of glue on the blue paper and sprinkle with gold glitter for the buttons on the jacket.
6. Repeat step 3 with the pink paper for the face and place it above the "jacket."
7. Glue two wiggly eyes on the pink paper and draw a nose and mouth on the face.
8. Turn the yogurt container upside down and have an adult use hot glue to attach the "hat" on the top end of the tube.
9. Glue small pieces of cotton below the edge of the hat for his hair and some on the face for his goatee.

Social Studies

83

www.harcourtschoolsupply.com
© Harcourt Achieve Inc. All rights reserved.

Social Studies Activities
Arts and Crafts Across the Curriculum 1, SV 1419023543

SEED PATTERNS

Use with "ABC Garden Cart" on page 4.

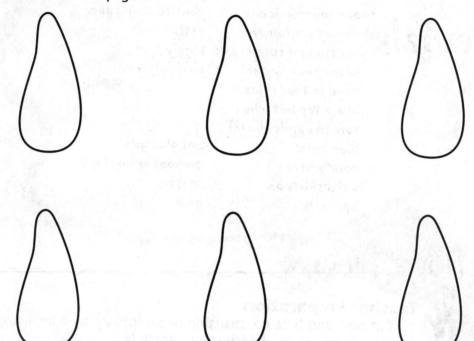

LEAF PATTERNS

Use with "Tube Tree with Root Words" on page 8.

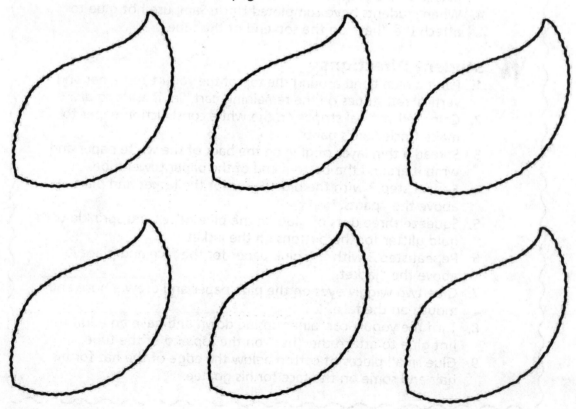

www.harcourtschoolsupply.com
© Harcourt Achieve Inc. All rights reserved.

Patterns
Arts and Crafts Across the Curriculum 1, SV 1419023543

SQUIRREL PATTERNS

Use with "Stand-Up Squirrel" on page 12.

www.harcourtschoolsupply.com
© Harcourt Achieve Inc. All rights reserved.

Patterns
Arts and Crafts Across the Curriculum 1, SV 1419023543

WING, NOUN, AND VERB PATTERNS

Use with "Tube Butterfly" on page 14.

www.harcourtschoolsupply.com
© Harcourt Achieve Inc. All rights reserved.

Patterns
Arts and Crafts Across the Curriculum 1, SV 1419023543

ANTHILL PATTERN

Use with "Cereal Box Anthill" on page 22.

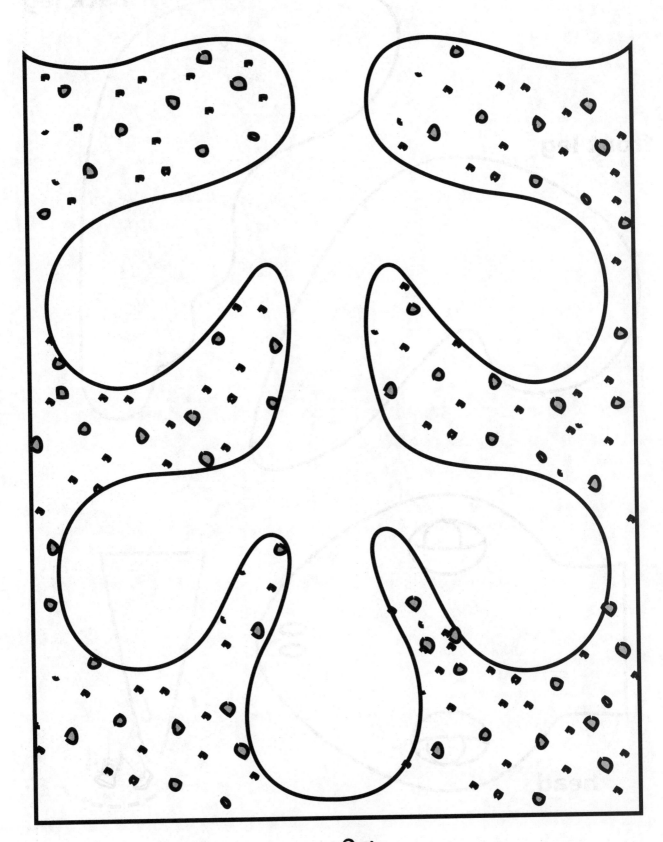

www.harcourtschoolsupply.com
© Harcourt Achieve Inc. All rights reserved.

Patterns
Arts and Crafts Across the Curriculum 1, SV 1419023543

TURTLE PATTERNS

Use with "Paper Plate Turtles" on page 24.

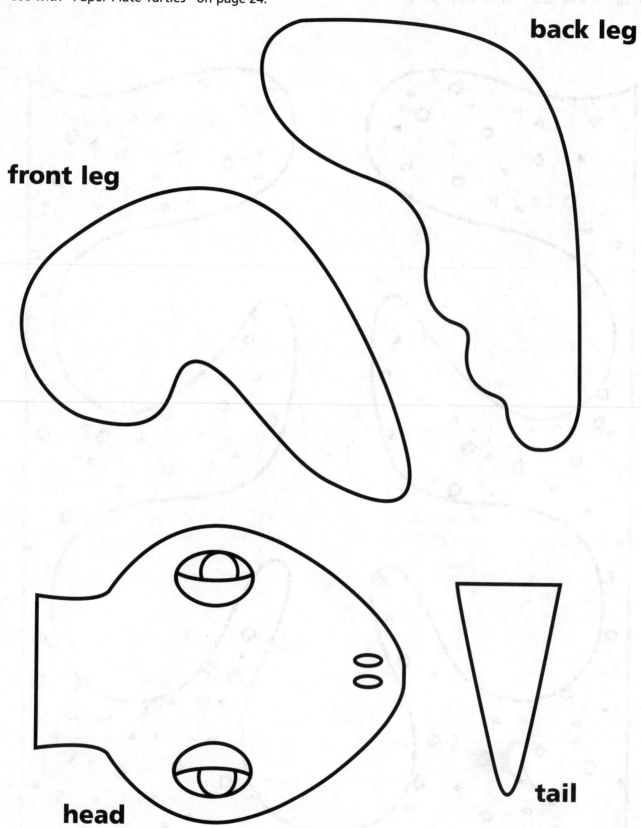

back leg

front leg

head

tail

www.harcourtschoolsupply.com
© Harcourt Achieve Inc. All rights reserved.

Patterns
Arts and Crafts Across the Curriculum 1, SV 1419023543

CLOCK PATTERNS

Use with "Ladybug Clock" on page 28.

www.harcourtschoolsupply.com
© Harcourt Achieve Inc. All rights reserved.

Patterns
Arts and Crafts Across the Curriculum 1, SV 1419023543

BIRD PATTERNS

Use with "Feathery Birds" on page 40.

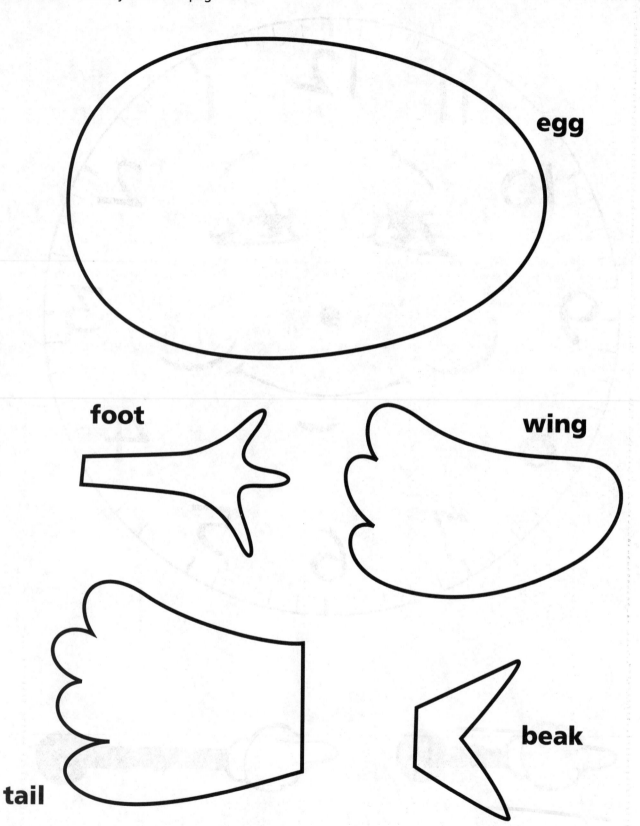

egg

foot

wing

tail

beak

www.harcourtschoolsupply.com
© Harcourt Achieve Inc. All rights reserved.

Patterns
Arts and Crafts Across the Curriculum 1, SV 1419023543

FROG PATTERNS

Use with "Frog on a Log" on page 46.

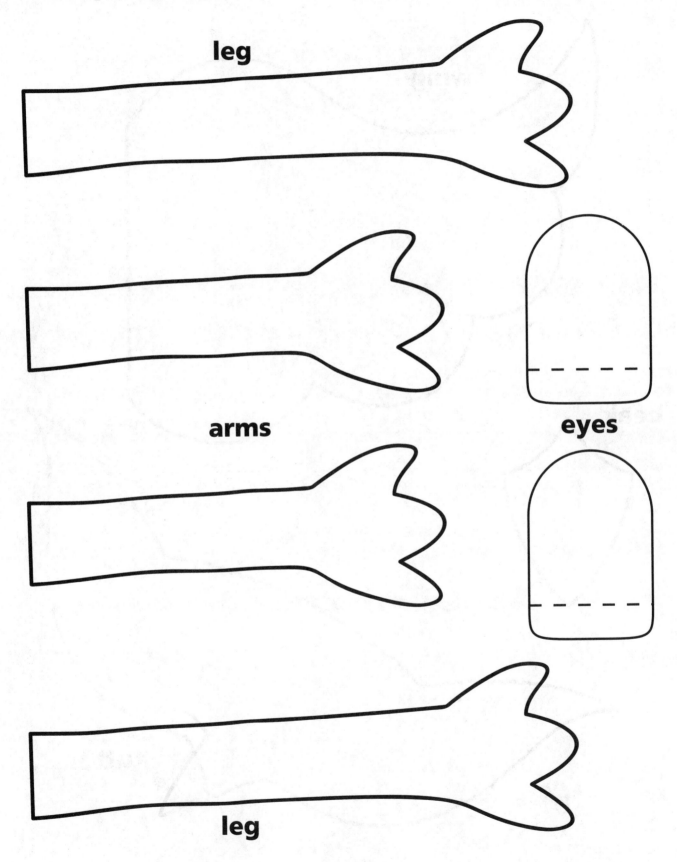

leg

arms

eyes

leg

91

www.harcourtschoolsupply.com
Patterns
Arts and Crafts Across the Curriculum 1, SV 1419023543

© Harcourt Achieve Inc. All rights reserved.

WING, BEAK, AND TUFT PATTERNS

Use with "Owl Puppet" on page 48.

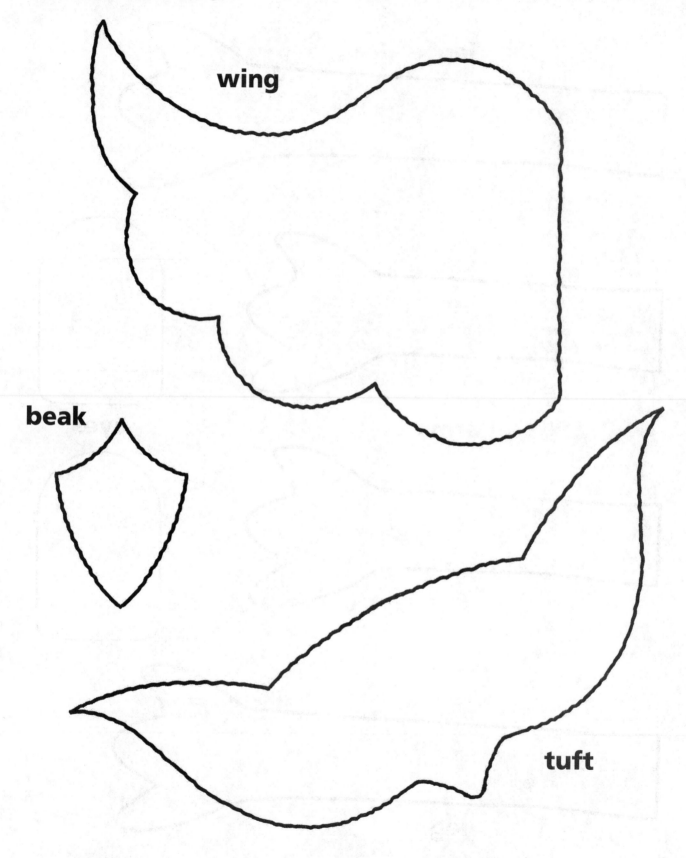

wing

beak

tuft

www.harcourtschoolsupply.com
© Harcourt Achieve Inc. All rights reserved.

Patterns
Arts and Crafts Across the Curriculum 1, SV 1419023543

BEAN SEED AND EMBRYO PATTERNS

Use with "Three-Part Seed" on page 50.

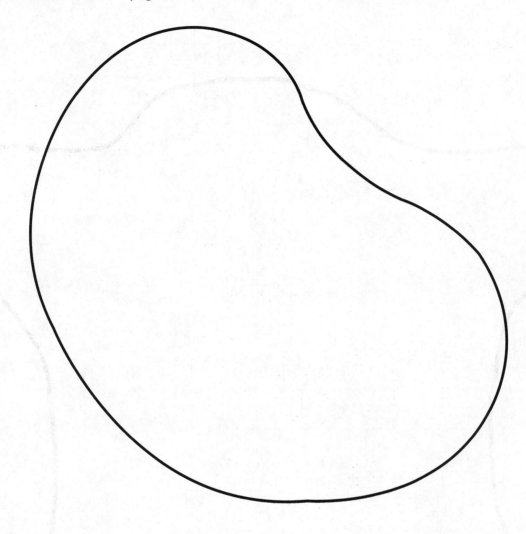

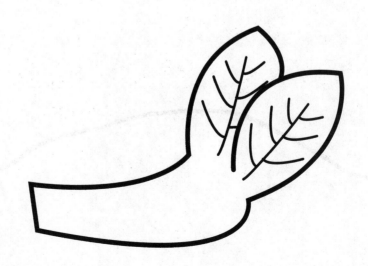

www.harcourtschoolsupply.com
© Harcourt Achieve Inc. All rights reserved.

Patterns
Arts and Crafts Across the Curriculum 1, SV 1419023543

BUFFALO SKIN PATTERN

Use with "Buffalo Skins" on page 74.

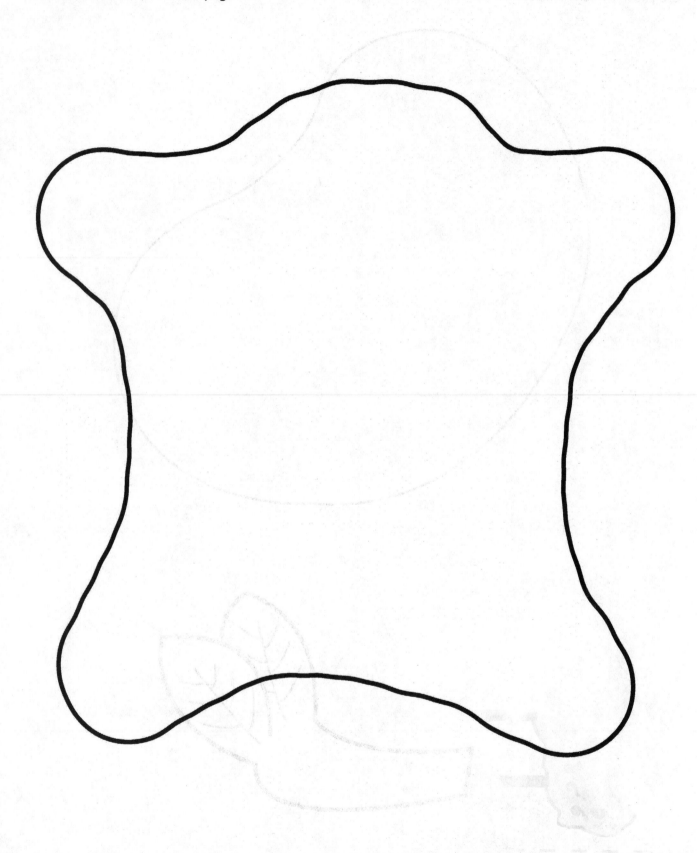

www.harcourtschoolsupply.com
© Harcourt Achieve Inc. All rights reserved.

Patterns
Arts and Crafts Across the Curriculum 1, SV 1419023543

JOHNNY APPLESEED PICTURES

Use with "Johnny Appleseed Story Wheel" on page 78.

www.harcourtschoolsupply.com
© Harcourt Achieve Inc. All rights reserved.

Patterns
Arts and Crafts Across the Curriculum 1, SV 1419023543

ALPHABETICAL INDEX

www.harcourtschoolsupply.com
© Harcourt Achieve Inc. All rights reserved.

Index
Arts and Crafts Across the Curriculum 1, SV 1419023543